Sing a Ne

Inspiring
Women
to go deeper with God

Sing a
New Song

Striking a new note in your relationship with God

Jeannette Barwick and Beverley Shepherd

Foreword by Elaine Storkey

See back of book for list of National Distributors.

Unless otherwise indicated, all Scripture references are from the Holy Bible: New International Version (NIV), copyright © 1973, 1978, 1984 by the International Bible Society.

Other versions used are marked:

NKJV: New King James Version, © 1982, Thomas Nelson Inc.

The Message: *The Message*, by Eugene Peterson, copyright © 1993, 1994, 1995, 1996, 2000, 2001, 2002. Used by permission of NavPress Publishing Group.

Concept development, editing, design and production by CWR

Front cover image: Artville: Don Bishop

Printed in Malta by Progress Press Ltd

ISBN: 1-85345-366-8

Contents

Meet the Women at Waverley Team

Jeannette Barwick, founder of Waverley's Ministry to Women, has long been committed to helping women apply biblical principles to their lives and relationships. In 1987, the first event for women was held at Waverley Abbey House and over the years the heart of Waverley's teaching for women has been shared around the world through seminars, writing and audio-cassettes. Jeannette also teaches on temperament differences and co-ordinates Selwyn Hughes' worldwide ministry.

Beth Clark, the most senior member of the team, is a lady whose life is steeped in the Scriptures. Her Bible Study has been ongoing for nearly 30 years and her workshops on Bible Meditation at Women at Waverley weekends are greatly prized. She has endeared herself to all who know her, not only by her humility and prayerfulness, but also by her remarkable ability to establish rapport with people of all ages.

Beverley Shepherd has been a team member for over ten years. She is involved in varied and demanding work as a training consultant. The encouraging and equipping of Christians in the workplace is one of her passions, and she is an associate speaker for the London Institute of Contemporary Christianity headed by Mark Greene. She brings to the team verve and vitality as well as depth of biblical understanding, and is especially appreciated for her ability to relate biblical truth to contemporary issues, particularly as they impact women.

Nicky-Sue Leonard is a a gifted teacher and a relative newcomer to the team, bringing to it her expertise and experience as a CWR-trained counsellor and facilitator of post-abortion workshops based on Christian principles. For a number of years she has co-ordinated women's events at Waverley and around the UK. Apart from an expanding role as a speaker at women's events, she is increasingly involved in teaching on CWR's counselling courses.

Foreword

For centuries people have gone to the book of Psalms and found wisdom. In the pages of these songs they have received encouragement, rebuke, joy, challenge and solace. In the Psalms people have found their own emotions laid bare, their own thankfulness expressed, their own confusion or anger scripted for them. There is a reality within the Psalms that speaks directly to people's hearts. For within them we do not find statements of glib piety or sentimentality. We find rugged faith which faces the realism of daily life and the profound questions of the human soul.

There are indeed great praise psalms: songs which express over-the-top exuberance, extolling the great majesty and power of the Creator. And many of them have been set to some of the finest music in history. There are songs of creation, where we see the world in its glory and beauty, as the detailed work of a loving God. There are songs of assurance and protection where our small lives are put in the perspective of the care of the Almighty. There are songs of redemption, where we are given hope for now and for eternity. There are so many psalms which make our hearts sing and our spirits soar.

But alongside the songs of thanksgiving and joy are those which also show us the depths of human grief and confusion. 'I had nearly lost confidence; my faith was almost gone' we are told in Psalm 73, 'because I was jealous of the proud when I saw that things go well for the wicked.' The honesty is brutal; the choices are stark. And there is little of human pain that is not here somewhere in the Psalms.

So the sheer scope of the Psalms is vast. That's why it cannot have been easy to choose just a few for this book. But the selection we have is inspired. For the ones included range over so many of the concerns of the whole. Creation, redemption, protection, direction, thankfulness are all themes which our two authors open up for us in the psalms of their choosing. And they open them up in a very personal way; we are taken into the lives of these two Christian women leaders as they share their insights with us. We hear their stories and learn from their experiences. Faithfully, they probe the texts and show us their relevance to our lives today.

For centuries people have gone to the Psalms to find wisdom. But more than that, they have gone to find God. This book plays its own part in making the search easier.

Elaine Storkey

Introduction

You and I are living in a time when many voices clamour for our attention and we need to know that it is God who is leading and directing our lives. The book of Psalms was written for just such a purpose. It is a book that helps us open up our hearts and hear from God.

In this book, *Sing a New Song*, we delve into seven of the psalms – songs of creation, redemption, delight, anger, protection, envy and thankfulness. Each psalm teaches us about a different aspect of God and how we might respond to Him.

The theme was initially explored over a women's weekend at Waverley Abbey House. As we spent time together in an inspirational and relaxing atmosphere, we were challenged to apply the truths of these psalms to our own lives, to discover the song we were currently singing to God in the varying circumstances of our lives and how we might sing a new song.

On the Saturday evening, participants were encouraged to choose from various options, including a time of silent reflection or writing their own psalm, their own message to God (some were set to music). Everyone was encouraged to be really honest before God.

At the end of the evening, we shared our experiences and sang several of these new psalms together. Here is one of them:

Oh the wondrous realisation
Lord, I am Yours.
Joy beyond all expectation,
Lord, I am Yours.
Others may despise, reject me
But I KNOW that You accept me,
And in love You will protect me,
Lord, I am Yours.

In Your hand my life You're holding
Lord, I am Yours.
Nothing from You now withholding
Lord, I am Yours.
Yours the praise for You are worthy,
Author of redemption's story,
This will be my theme in Glory
Lord, I am Yours.

Even greater Truth I mention,
Lord, You are mine.
Oh, what loving condescension!
Lord, You are mine.
Your redeeming love has sealed it,
The Holy Spirit has revealed it,
Totally to You I'm yielded,
Lord, You are mine.

Once more Beverley Shepherd and I bring you the heart of the
weekend's teaching. There are questions for reflection at the end
of each chapter and our prayer is that, as you progress through the
book, you too will experience God's presence, God's power and God's
provision and be enabled to sing a new song to Him through your
life.

Jeannette Barwick
Waverley Abbey House
July 2005

Chapter One

A Song of Creation

Psalm 139

Jeannette Barwick

'O Lᴏʀᴅ, you have searched me and you know me.
You know when I sit and when I rise;
you perceive my thoughts from afar.'

(Psalm 139:1–2)

Psalm 139 is one of the most cherished and beautiful of all the psalms. It is attributed to David, who wrote the majority of the psalms, and is one of the most personal passages in the whole of Scripture. It is all about God's continual, active presence with us wherever we go, day or night. It makes it clear that He is constantly watching over us and thinking about us. He knows us and we can know Him.

One of the key thoughts in the Old Testament is the idea of knowing God. God said through Jeremiah, 'Let not the wise man glory in his wisdom, Let not the mighty man glory in his might, Nor let the rich man glory in his riches; But let him who glories glory in this, That he understands and knows Me' (Jer. 9:23–24, NKJV). God says the one thing that we can take pride in is the fact that we know Him. Following this same line of thought, Jesus said, 'And this is eternal life, that they may know You, the only true God, and Jesus Christ whom You have sent' (John 17:3, NKJV). So, eternal life is based on whether or not we've come to know God.

There are many more passages that convey the same thought but I want to suggest to you now that it's possible for a person to know a great deal about God without ever knowing God. And I think that, too often, we've confused the two. We may manage to come up with a list of God's qualities – He's eternal, holy, all-loving, all-wise, omnipotent (all-powerful), omniscient (all-knowing), omnipresent (everywhere at the same time) – and conclude that, if we can identify all these attributes of God, then we know Him. But that's knowing *about* God which doesn't mean that we really know Him.

You may know, for example, that my name is Jeannette Barwick, that I've worked for CWR for over 20 years and head up the Ministry to Women; that I co-ordinate Selwyn Hughes' ministry and have travelled to many different countries with the CWR team. Those who have heard me teach will know I have several grandchildren because

I love to talk about them. But knowing all that doesn't mean that you know me. It merely means that you know something about me.

To know God is not just to have an intellectual knowledge about God: it's to have an intimate personal relationship with Him as the most important relationship in our life.

In his book *Knowing God*, the theologian Jim Packer writes, 'What matters supremely, therefore, is not in the last analysis the fact that I know God, but the larger fact which underlies it – the fact that *He knows me*. We are graven on the palms of God's hands and never out of the Divine mind. All our knowledge of God depends on God's sustained initiative in knowing us. We know God because God first knew us and continues to know us.'

I heard about a young man who had spent his whole life collecting Elvis memorabilia. Elvis Presley was his hero. He bought his clothes, records and photographs. He even underwent plastic surgery to try to look more like him. But his great regret was that he never got to meet the man he adored.

A similar but greater tragedy with many Christians is that they spend years listening to sermons, reading the Scriptures, maybe even teaching Bible classes, while failing to enjoy a close relationship with God.

Having considered the importance of our knowing God, let us observe that Psalm 139 opens with a reminder that God already knows us. Even before we know God, even before we make the effort to begin to know God, He knows us inside and out.

God knows us (vv.1–6)

I want you to think for a moment about what would it be like for somebody to know everything about you. Do you think you'd like that? It's not unusual to hear someone complain, 'Nobody really knows me, nobody understands me.' And it's true that there is generally a shallowness to our relationships. When someone asks how we're doing, the socially acceptable answer is 'Fine.' Inside we may be thinking, 'My boss is being impossible, my children are driving me up the wall, I can't take any more,' but we say, 'I'm doing fine.' And we smile.

In Psalm 139:1–6, David wrote, 'O LORD, you have searched me and you know me. You know when I sit and when I rise; you perceive my thoughts from afar. You discern my going out and my lying down; you are familiar with all my ways. Before a word is on my tongue, you know it completely, O LORD. You hem me in – behind and before; you have laid your hand upon me. Such knowledge is too wonderful for me, too lofty for me to attain.'

David writes descriptively about how God knows us. And it's not just that God knows everything. We sometimes say that God is omniscient, that is, knowing everything there is to know, and that's certainly true. You can read, in Job chapters 38 and 39, where God is speaking to Job and says to him, 'Do you know how the foundations of the earth were laid and do you know how the sun sits in the sky and do you know how this happens and that happens?' Job's answer must obviously be 'No.' And the implication is that God does know all that. He knows everything.

But that's not David's point here. It is not that God knows all the mysteries of history and the riddles of the universe but rather that He knows every single person in His creation. He knows everything there is to be known about us. And in desiring to know God, we need to be fully aware of the fact that He knows us before we can know Him.

David uses six terms to describe the fact that God knows us:

1. God has searched me

The Hebrew term here originally meant to explore, and sometimes conveyed the idea of digging into something. It's the word used in Judges 18 for spying out the land, and in Job 28 for digging for mineral ore. It's a way of looking intently. David says here, 'God, you have searched me …' Have you lost anything recently – keys, wallet, remote control for the TV, your glasses? When you misplace something, you go all over, looking desperately, turning things upside down. Looking here, there, looking everywhere. And that's the word David uses here: 'O LORD, you have searched me.' God looks intently into my life. God looks intently into your life.

2. He knows me

Verse 1 says, '… you know me'. Verse 2 repeats this: 'You know when I sit and when I rise.' This is not 'know' in the sense of just knowing something *about* us but knowing me in the sense that my best friend knows me. God knows me more than I can even imagine, and maybe more that I want at times. Whether I'm taking it easy or whether I'm on the move, it makes no difference: God knows me. And God knows you.

3. He understands my thoughts

The latter part of verse 2: 'you perceive my thoughts from afar.' The idea is that God can get inside my head. He can see what's going on there. Doctors can do some amazing things with the technology that's available today. They can take a tube and stick it down your throat and look at your insides. That's amazing. But magnify that a billion times. You've got God seeing everything inside, not just my physical body but even my thoughts. God knows everything I've ever thought about.

4. He comprehends my comings and goings

The beginning of verse 3: 'You comprehend my path and my lying down …' (NKJV). God examines us thoroughly.

5. He is familiar with my ways

The end of verse 3: '… you are familiar with all my ways.' It comes out just a little bit stronger maybe in the Hebrew: 'I can't get away with anything' is a loose translation. God knows my habits, my strengths, my weaknesses. He knows all my business.

6. He knows my words before they're on my tongue

Perhaps most amazing of all is verse 4: 'Before a word is on my tongue, you know it completely.' Even before I speak a word, God knows what I'm going to say. Have you ever been so close to somebody that they know what you're going to say even before you say it? I know that I sometimes start a sentence and one of my daughters will finish it for me; they know what I'm going to say. It's that way and even more so with God. In Matthew 10:30, Jesus said, 'And even the very hairs of your head are all numbered.' It is not that God concerns Himself with trivia but simply that He's all-knowing and therefore aware of everything we do and everything we think. He knows what goes on in private as well as what we do in public. Even our deepest, seemingly hidden, motives are known by our all-knowing God.

Verse 6, loosely translated, says, 'That blows me away!' Trying to comprehend that God knows us, scrutinises us, studies us 24 hours a day, 'blows our minds'.

Does that realisation arouse mixed emotions in you?

Trying to hide from God (vv.7–12)

Where, should we wish to, can we hide from God's penetrating gaze? 'Where can I go from your Spirit?' says David. 'Where can I flee from your presence?' These rhetorical questions are an emphatic way of declaring that God's presence is everywhere. While David may have wanted to run from God at different points in his life, he understands that there is nowhere to go to get away from Him. Since God is Spirit, He can invade our physical being. It is impossible to get away from Him. In verse 8, David contemplates what would happen if he tried to go up to the heavens: heaven is a vast place and yet offers no way of escaping God. The phrase 'in the depths' refers to Sheol which, in the Bible, is the realm of the dead. Throughout the Bible two places are contrasted: heaven, a place of light and life, and Sheol, a place of darkness and death.

God is present in the upper regions of the world and in the depths of the earth. (The word 'You' is very emphatic and impressive in the original text and one has to shout it out to get the meaning: YOU! GOD! YOU are there!)

After checking out the heights and the depths, David decided to travel from east to west. In verse 9, he met the dawn and travelled with the sun to the far side of the sea. God was there! The phrase he uses, the 'wings of the dawn', is an elegant metaphor referring to the sunbeams that flash out from the sun in the morning. They appear swiftly and just as quickly disappear. David is saying that if he could just pluck these wings of the dawn and travel as far and as fast as light, even there God would be with him. Verse 10 provides David some comfort: wherever he ends up, God's hand will guide and protect him. It was impossible to run so far away that he would be out of the reach of God.

I've been to Australia and New Zealand a few times. They are the farthest points on the planet to which I could ever go from my home but, when I am there, I am always comforted by the thought that even on the far side of the ocean, on the other side of the world, God is still there with me.

Jonah found this out the hard way. We read in chapter 1 of the book of Jonah that he was commissioned by God to go and preach to the great city of Nineveh. He was to tell them how wicked they were. Jonah didn't like his assignment. So what did he do? He tried to flee the presence of the Lord. He jumped on a ship to Tarshish but that didn't help – although he could run away from what God had asked him to do, he couldn't hide from God Himself. Jonah probably heaved a sigh of relief when the ship sailed away from the shore; he thought he was in the clear, that he had outwitted God. But what Jonah found out was that God was with him on the ship, and would soon be with him in the belly of the big fish. We cannot run from God because there's no place to hide. Like David, Jonah investigated the heights and the depths, the East and the West, the land and the sea, and he could not find a place where God was not present. Wherever Jonah went, God's hand was there to guide him, His right hand holding him fast.

In Psalm 139:11 we see that David started to wonder what difference it might make if it were day or night: 'If I say, "Surely the darkness will hide me and the light become night around me …"' David was playing around with the idea that darkness might enable him to be out of God's reach.

I can remember playing hide and seek with my two daughters when they were little and how, when it was their turn to hide, they would stand in the middle of the room with their eyes closed and their hands over their face. They thought that if they couldn't see me, then I couldn't see them! It was dark to them, but it was light to me.

That's the way it is with us and God. We think that we're hiding things from Him just because it's dark, or we think we're doing something in secret, but God sees everything because He is present everywhere at the same time. He is always present whether we believe it or not. He is always available to us wherever we go, 24 hours a day. The phrase 24/7 really belongs to God. There is no place you or I can go and find that God is not there and has not been there, waiting for us to arrive.

The truth of God's omnipresence can be soothing or unsettling. To some it brings comfort. Others find it very convicting. Those who find it convicting may, like Jonah, be trying to run from God. All I can say is, 'Don't wait until God sends a storm into your life, or you'll end up with a whale of a problem! Stop running right now!'

Hebrews 4:13 puts it all into perspective: 'Nothing in all creation is hidden from God's sight. Everything is uncovered and laid bare before the eyes of him to whom we must give account.' Are you doing something right now in secret? Maybe you think that no one else will find out. Perhaps you've arranged everything so that you can get away with it. Friends, there is no way you and I can avoid the presence of God. He sees what we're doing because He's with us. No matter what we might think, there is nothing we can get away with. Even our most deeply-hidden motives are known by our all-knowing God. If the Holy Spirit is convicting you, then this is a wonderful opportunity to get alone with God, ask His forgiveness and cleansing and be restored to a right relationship with Him. You can be confident, if He is convicting you, it is because He loves you.

For the follower of Christ there is comfort. There is a sense of joyful calmness in knowing that everywhere we go, no matter what happens, God is watching over us. I often thank Him for His watchful care over me each day. It is a tremendous blessing to realise that, even if no other person in the world notices my trials, anguish, pain or discouragement, God knows … He sees!

Fearfully and wonderfully made (vv.13–18)

In a TV sitcom, a teenager, having an argument with his father, says, 'I didn't ask to be born!' To which the father replies 'If you had, I would've said no!' How sad! The truth is, none of us had any say in our conception, and the creation of a human life is a miraculous, divine action. Every human life is an extension of the work of the Creator.

David acknowledged that God was there before he was born, that His Spirit was right there as he was formed in his mother's womb. He was so impressed with the wonder of God's gift of life that he spoke of being 'woven together', using the imagery of a craftsman by whom he was 'fearfully and wonderfully made'.

Human beings, I believe, exist from the moment of conception and not, as some believe, from when they take their first breath of air. Couples may say a baby is an 'accident' or a 'mistake', but God does not. God is present and by this work God reveals His glory. This word 'fearfully' in verse 14 could be translated as 'reverently', implying that the forming of life is a sacred act.

Through the wonders of modern technology, scans can now show us the amazing pre-natal development of a baby. I found it incredibly moving to be with my pregnant daughter at her 16-week scan as together we watched her precious baby moving in her womb.

The fact that God created us is the reason He knows us so well. He lovingly formed every molecule of which you are composed. Your body is an intricate weaving from the dust bearing the divine image. Someone once 'did the maths' on our bodies and came up with the amazing facts that, every day, your heart beats 104,178 times, your blood travels 171,000 miles, you breathe 23,172 times inhaling 438 cubic feet of air, you move 752 major muscles and exercise 8,000,000 brain cells. We do this every day!

Augustine once said, 'People travel to wonder at the height of mountains, at the huge waves of the sea, at the circular motion of the stars and they pass by themselves without wondering.' He was right. Sometimes, we don't think of ourselves as being wonderfully made. There is the temptation to let the things of this sinful planet determine who and what is wonderful and it is very easy to fall into thinking that way, too.

How many of us have the idea that, because we are not outstanding in our field of work or sport, and not the sort of genius that collects multiple doctorates, we are a little less wonderfully made than those capable of such achievements? But, when it comes to creation, we are all God's 'works of art' (Eph. 2:10), crafted as His unique creations. We forget that God is the artist and we are His artwork, each of us bearing His image. David arrived at the conclusion that he was a valuable individual because he recognised that he was created by God. It was God who gave his life value and worth and God gives value and worth to the life of every follower of Jesus Christ.

Verse 15 tells us God was there when we were being formed in the secret place and verse 16 that all our days were written in His book before any one came to be. It's all so incredibly intimate and individual and personal!

What does this mean to us now, today, personally? To help us enter into the truth of this, I want you to fill out the name and address section on the next page and, like youngsters at school, write your country before the world, the universe, and in the last line 'the mind of God'. Gaze at this and, as you do so, meditate also on the scripture that reminds us we were 'chosen in him before the creation of the world' (Eph. 1:4).

Name _____

Address _____

_____

Country _____

… The World
The Universe
The Mind of God

Your life is a miracle. God created you and knew you from the moment of your conception. You are no accident. You are part of His overall plan. He has created you to be someone completely unique. No one else smiles, talks or thinks the way you do. He delights in you.

All the way through this wonderful psalm we are made aware that God is constantly watching over and thinking about us. David said, 'How precious to me are your thoughts, O God! How vast is the sum of them! Were I to count them, they would outnumber the grains of sand' (vv.17–18). Can you guess how many grains of sand are on the seashores of the world?

The same thought that went into the construction of the created world has gone also into the plan of salvation. I imagine that God thinks about His redeemed children more than He does about the material universe. To create the world He simply spoke, but to save us He had to give His one and only Son to die on a cross. The humblest soul means more to Him than a million galaxies. God is saying to you and me, 'You are always on my mind. I am always thinking about you.'

As I was preparing this talk for the first women's weekend at Waverley on this theme, Susan Lenzkes' poem for inclusion in *Every Day with Jesus* arrived by email. It expresses so beautifully what it means to find our identity in God that I would like to share it with you.

Identity

On the night that I was born
Into your family, Lord,
Did You dance upon
The rain-slicked streets,
Full of grace and joy at the potential and pure eternal life
You had birthed in me?
Dipping a sacred finger into
Your Son's sacrificial love, You
Traced my form from the
Well of Your divine intention.
And then You called me
Your Beloved in Christ,
Whispering that I would grow up
To be like Him one day.
Oh Father, can it be that
This is who I really am?

Susan Lenzkes © 2004[1]

The enemies of God (vv.19–22)

David's zeal for God sets him against all God's adversaries. He will not team up with those who hate God or who are actively sinning against Him.

Search me, O God (vv.23–24)

'Search me … and know my heart' are words that could only be spoken by someone who feels completely loved and accepted. These words could only be spoken to someone who unconditionally loves the person he is watching.

Psalm 139 describes not the eye of a critic that is searching for an opportunity to put you down. Rather it is the eye of a loving parent or a true friend.

It has been said that a friend is someone who knows all about you and loves you just the same. A wonderful hymn talks about that type of friendship: *What a friend we have in Jesus* has the lines, 'Jesus knows our every weakness, take it to the Lord in prayer'; and 'In His arms He'll take and shield thee, thou wilt find a solace there'. God knows us fully and loves us unconditionally. Even in moments of the utmost penetration we know that He looks on us with eyes of love.

Spend time with the One who made you. He will reveal the person He made you to be and He will help you to attain all He has called you to be. May your song of response to Him take on a new note.

Questions for reflection

- Could you honestly claim to know God rather than to know about Him? If the answer is 'No', ask Him now to give you the heart's desire to know Him as He wants to be known and to make it the central reality of your life.

- Make a list of those things you do know about God. Which of His attributes mean the most to you and why?

- How do you feel about being known completely by God? Is there some secret you would like to bring into the open with Him, confessing your foolishness in trying to hide it from Him?

- Could your relationships with some people be described as 'shallow'? Would you like to change this and how might you go about it?

- Can you think of a way in which you, like Jonah, might be trying to hide or run away from God? What help do you need, and how will you get it, to carry through what He wants you to do?

- When does God feel least near to you? When does He seem most close? How might you enjoy more of His close presence?

- How and when do you lose sight of the fact that you are God's precious 'work of art'? What things about you do you find it hard to thank Him for? Could you do so now, regardless?

Notes

1. The poem *Identity* by Susan Lenzkes, first published in *Every Day with Jesus* May/June 2005. Used by permission.

Chapter Two

A Song of Redemption

Psalm 40

Beverley Shepherd
Original talk given by Nicky-Sue Leonard

'He put a new song in my mouth,
a hymn of praise to our God.
Many will see and fear
and put their trust in the Lord.'

(Psalm 40:3)

salm 40 is a song of redemption. Redemption means the deliverance from captivity or some evil by the payment of a price. For redemption to happen there has to be a redeemer – one who is willing to pay the price. The story is told of a fine Negro slave being sold at auction in America before the days of abolition. The bidding for this slave was being led by a foreign-looking man. The slave began to curse the man saying, 'If you buy me, I will never work for you. I would sooner die than work for you. If you buy me I'll try to kill you!' He knew that if he were bought by a foreign buyer he'd be separated from his relatives and most likely never see them again.

But still the man went on bidding, consistently increasing his offer with every counter bid, and eventually the slave was sold to him. He paid the money over to the auctioneer, received the bill of sale, and walked over to the slave. As he approached he stretched out his hand with the bill of sale in it. 'Take it,' he said, 'you're a free man.' The slave looked blank for a moment, and then fell on his knees before this unknown benefactor. 'Sir,' he said, 'I will serve you and go with you wherever you want. Your home will be my home; your concerns my concerns, and your wish my command. I am yours.'[1]

The story of this slave is but a pale reflection of the story of our redemption – a story told by Psalm 40. This psalm, written by David, is a journey and together we will explore each stage of that journey. It is a journey:

From slimy pit to firm rock
From helpless cry to new song
From vain pride to obedient trust
From desperation to proclamation
From past to present, and
From present to future.

From slimy pit to firm rock

David depicts his situation as a slimy pit full of mud and mire. We do not know exactly what this represented, whether it was disease, depression, sin or persecution, but we can identify with the helplessness of his situation. There is no climbing out of a slimy pit – every attempt to haul yourself out leaves you slipping back into the mud.

Although David is unlikely to be referring to an actual pit, Joseph, Jeremiah and Daniel all found themselves in such a place. Joseph was thrown into a cistern by his brothers who were jealous of him and hated his dreams (Gen. 37:24). Jeremiah was lowered into a muddy cistern because he dared to declare the message God had given him – that Babylon would capture the city (Jer. 38:1–13). Daniel refused to stop praying to God three times a day, despite the king's edict, and found himself in a pit occupied by lions as a result (Dan. 6). In each situation they were totally helpless and reliant on God.

Though they may not be as dramatic as any of theirs, we all face situations over which we have no control. I remember the time that I had purchased a computer by mail order from a firm in London. In the first two weeks I had one problem after another until the machine just died on me. Phone calls to the company had not achieved anything other than frustration. I was left holding on the line for 20 minutes or more and when I eventually spoke to their finance manager was told, 'Let's face it lady, we've got your money!' I went to church that Sunday with a heavy heart, not knowing what to do – I needed a computer for my work and could not afford to buy another one. Our minister preached on 2 Chronicles 20:12: 'We do not know what to do, but our eyes are upon you.' Was Jesus interested in my computer? Could God really change the attitude of a computer company? Yes, but He had to change me first! He enabled me to let go of my anger and frustration and to trust. I drove up to London the next day with my computer and waited patiently for half an hour before someone would see me. In the end it was the finance manager who came down to reception! He offered to have the machine repaired but I just quietly asked for my money back instead. He agreed!

What should be our response when we find ourselves 'in the pit'? To cry out and to wait patiently. I do not find it easy to ask for help and yet God longs that we should bring all our concerns to Him. Looking again at the hymn *What a friend we have in Jesus* it puts it:

> O what peace we often forfeit
> O what needless pain we bear,
> All because we do not carry
> Everything to God in prayer![2]

And then we await His answer – trusting in His provision and His timing. Verse 2 of Psalm 40 shows us God's response – He hears our cry, He turns (literally 'bends down') to me, He lifts me out of the muddy pit and then He sets my feet on a firm rock. In the Old Testament 'rock' symbolises security and safety.

Corrie ten Boom tells of making her way to a Christian hospital in Holland called the Deaconess House, after her release from Ravensbrück concentration camp. 'I was then taken to a cosy bedroom so I could rest. How lovely was the combination of colours. I was starved for colour. In the concentration camp everything was grey. But here in Holland the colours were vivid again. My eyes could not seem to get enough to satisfy them. And the bed! Delightfully soft and clean with thick woollen blankets. One of the little nurses brought an extra pillow and tucked it under my swollen feet. I wanted to laugh and cry all at the same time … Only to those who have been in prison does freedom have such a great meaning.'[3] Corrie had been lifted from the pit of Ravensbrück to the rock of Deaconess House.

From helpless cry to new song

What is the cry that comes from your life and mine? What do those listening to our lives day by day actually hear? If we stop and listen to the cry of our friends, neighbours, work colleagues or people we pass in the street we will hear a strange medley of songs: songs of pain, of selfishness, of desolation, of hopelessness, of fear and of loneliness. I was moved when I heard Bette Midler singing *Hello in there* – the lyrics paint the sad picture of a woman whose children have left home, whose marriage is empty and whose life is without hope. The song's refrain is:

> You know that old trees just grow stronger,
> and old rivers grow wilder every day,
> but old people, they just grow lonesome
> waiting for someone to say,
> 'Hello in there. Hello.'[4]

What saddened me was the realisation that many people sing this song of quiet desperation.

Sometimes we use a louder song to drown out the painful music of our hearts – a song of anger to cover up our pain, a song of busyness to cover up our loneliness, a song of achievement and success to cover up our emptiness, a song of pride to cover our insecurity, or a song of strength to cover our vulnerability. Whatever other people hear, Jesus hears the real song that our lives are singing – He hears the helpless cry. Often, before giving us a new song to sing, He waits for us to listen to ourselves – to turn down the volume on the cover-up song and face the reality of the helpless cry.

How do we listen? One way is the Prayer of Examen, described by Richard Foster as follows: 'It has two basic aspects, like the two sides of a door. The first is an *examen of consciousness* through which we discover how God has been present to us throughout the day and how we have responded to his loving presence. The second aspect is an *examen of conscience* in which we uncover those areas that need cleansing, purifying and healing.'[5] I have found as I reflect back over the day, asking God to review it with me from His perspective, that I have a changed view on what was important. I become aware of His presence and provision during the day and sometimes He highlights one seemingly trivial smile or comment as important, at other times He shows me an attitude that requires repentance. I remember, on one occasion, whilst praying on the way back from a meeting of training consultants, God showed me how hurtful my dismissive comment to one man must have been. As soon as I got home I emailed him and apologised.

It is only when we have acknowledged that we are in a slimy pit and need His help to get out that He can give us a new song. What is this new song? It is a song of praise. 'He put a new song in my mouth, a hymn of praise to our God. Many will see and fear and put their trust in the LORD' (v.3).

Corrie ten Boom continues the story of her time at Deaconess House with these words: 'I knew my life had been given back for a purpose. I was no longer my own. This time I had been ransomed and released. I knew that God would soon be sending me out as a tramp for the Lord. But right now, He was letting me enjoy the luxury of thanksgiving. I was drinking from a fountain I knew would never run dry – the fountain of praise.'[6] We explore the whole theme of praise more fully in Chapter Six.

From vain pride to obedient trust

'Blessed is the man who makes the LORD his trust, who does not look to the proud, to those who turn aside to false gods' (v.4).

Christianity is unique in the emphasis it puts on pride and its converse, humility – it is unparalleled in other religious or ethical systems. 'Rebellious pride, which refuses to depend on God and be subject to him, but attributes to self the honour due him, figures as the very root and essence of sin.'[7]

People believed the *Titanic* to be unsinkable. On 10 April 1912, as the passengers embarked on the liner's maiden voyage, one of the crew said to a lady who expressed her nervousness, 'Madam, even God Himself could not sink this ship.' Yet when they were 500 miles south of Newfoundland the liner struck a huge iceberg, tearing a 300-foot-long hole in her side. She sank with the loss of many lives.[8]

Have you ever believed yourself to be unsinkable? Do you strive to keep everything under control (ie, *your* control)? Do you look to some strategy other than God to make your life work? Sometimes it takes a slimy pit or icy waters to rid us of our pride. I believe God has allowed many of the difficult situations in my life for just such a purpose – to cause me to turn from proudly relying on my own self-help strategies and to cry out to Him. Well can I identify with Paul when he says: 'Indeed, in our hearts we felt the sentence of death. But this happened that we might not rely on ourselves but on God, who raises the dead' (2 Cor. 1:9).

What is the antidote? The humility that leads to obedient trust! The Hebrew and Greek words for obey mean 'hearken to' and 'hear under'. The idea of obedience which this vocabulary suggests is of a listening that takes place under the authority of the speaker (God) and that leads to compliance with His requests. No wonder Psalm 40:6 says '… my ears you have pierced …' (literally 'dug out'). One friend of mine refused to have his ears tested, claiming that he wasn't deaf, even though he frequently asked for things to be repeated or misunderstood what had been said. He was too proud to acknowledge that he needed a hearing aid. Others of us have 'selective deafness' – we only choose to hear those things that comply with our world-view.

Hearing, in the Bible, always assumes obedience. Past disobedience can block our ability to hear God in the present, in which case we need to ask God to dig out our ears through repentance.

Obedience is not meant to be a hard task but a joyful response to the grace we have received – His Law is now written on our hearts. 'I desire to do your will, O my God; your law is within my heart' (v.8).

From desperation to proclamation

Our proclamation is twofold – through our lives and with our lips. 'Many will see and fear and put their trust in the LORD' (v.3). What do people see when they observe your life and mine? Is it something that would cause them to trust God? The story is told of a young black boy in South Africa under apartheid. He was walking beside his mother when a tall white man greeted them by raising his hat. The boy was amazed that a white man should raise his hat to a black woman. 'Why did he do that?' he asked his mother. 'Because he is a priest,' was her reply. 'I want to be a priest,' the boy said. The tall white man was Trevor Huddlestone, then a parish priest in the black Johannesburg suburb of Sophiatown and a tireless opponent of apartheid. The name of the young black boy was Desmond Tutu.[9] My prayer is that my life speaks before I open my mouth.

Yet we are required to open our mouths. 'I proclaim righteousness in the great assembly; I do not seal my lips, as you know, O LORD. I do not hide your righteousness in my heart; I speak of your faithfulness and salvation. I do not conceal your love and your truth from the great assembly' (vv.9–10).

Many of us shrink from speaking about Jesus – I find Esther a helpful role model here. When she explains to her uncle Mordecai that if she approaches the king without his permission she may be killed, his reply is:

'Do not think that because you are in the king's house you alone of all the Jews will escape. For if you remain silent at this time, relief and deliverance for the Jews will arise from another place, but you and your father's family will perish. And who knows but that you have come to royal position for such a time as this?' (Esth. 4:13–14)

Esther's reaction to this challenge is instructive: (a) She prays and asks for others to pray; (b) She dresses in her royal robes – we are daughters of the King and do not need to be ashamed; (c) Despite the king's extravagant promise, she does not take advantage of the situation by mentioning the edict. This would have embarrassed him in front of the whole court; (d) She restores relationship by inviting him to dinner, twice; (e) She awaits the right time before making her request; (f) She does not allow fear of death to prevent her from speaking.

My own experience is that as I have prayed and asked others to pray, then opportunities to speak about my faith come. I would like to be able to say that I always take those opportunities, but that is not the case. Yet God is faithful, even when I am not, and, as I repent of my silence, He gives new opportunities to speak.

From past to present

It is as the psalmist looks back to God's past deliverance that he has confidence that God will help him in his present circumstances. We learn that 'troubles without number surround me; my sins have overtaken me, and I cannot see. They are more than the hairs of my head, and my heart fails within me' (v.12). David is quite clear that the cause of his trouble is his own sin – sin that he acknowledges before God. He is literally heartbroken over his sin.

God never despises 'a broken and contrite heart,' says the psalmist

(Psa. 51:17). But the real question for us in the modern world is how do we experience a contrite heart, a grieving, broken, sorrowing, repentant heart? We begin by asking. We simply cannot make heart repentance happen … it is a gift from God, pure and simple. If at first heart sorrow does not come we keep asking, we keep seeking, and we keep knocking.[10]

When we fully grasp hold of the fact that our sin blocks our relationship with God, then the only appropriate response is deep sorrow. Yet confession brings forgiveness and once again we are lifted out of the slimy pit.

From present to future

The psalm ends with a contrast between two different kinds of 'seeker': those who *seek to take my life* and those *who seek you* – between the godly and the ungodly. The ungodly betray their ungodliness in their persecution of the godly and in their lack of acknowledgment of their need of a redeemer. Our eternal future depends on the choice as to which type of seeker we will be in this life. Can we say with the psalmist: 'Yet I am poor and needy; may the Lord think of me. You are my help and my deliverer; O my God, do not delay' (v.17).

Whatever the song of our lives has been up to this point, God can put a new song in our mouths – a song that proclaims His deliverance and His praise, a song that declares our desire to do His will and humbly follow Him; a song that acknowledges our sin in the assurance of His mercy, and a song that knows His eternal plans for us – yes, a song of redemption!

Questions for reflection

- In what areas of your life are you aware of the need to cry out, 'I don't know what to do, but my eyes are on you'?

- What is the song that people hear when listening to your life? Use the Prayer of Examen to help discern this.

- Are you aware of any areas of pride, or of disobedience in your life?

- If God gives you awareness of pride or disobedience ask Him for a contrite and broken heart.

- Who might God be asking you to speak to about Him?

- Take time to pray for those you know and love who do not yet know God's redemption.

Notes
1. Simon Coupland, *A Dose of Salts* (Monarch Books, 1997), adapted from a talk by Peter Sertin, Paris, 1981.
2. Joseph M. Scriven, from the *Methodist Hymn Book*.
3. Corrie ten Boom, *Tramp for the Lord* (Hodder & Stoughton, 1974), p.26.
4. John Prime (Sour Grapes Music/Walden Music, Inc, ASCAP)
5. Richard Foster, *Prayer* (Hodder & Stoughton, 1992), pp.27–28.
6. Corrie ten Boom, *op. cit.*, p.27.
7. Howard I. Marshall, et al. (editors), *New Bible Dictionary* (IVP, 1962), p. 966.
8. Simon Coupland, *op. cit.*, adapted from *Headlines*, issue 1.
9. Simon Coupland, *op. cit.*, adapted from a talk by Brother Bernard, 1992.
10. Richard Foster, *op. cit.*, p.43.

Chapter Three

A Song of Delight

Psalm 119

Jeannette Barwick
Original talk given by Beth Clark

'Your word is a lamp to my feet and a light for my path.'

(Psalm 119:105)

Psalm 119 celebrates the dynamic power of God's Word in the life of the believer. It is the longest of all the psalms (in fact, twice the length of the next longest and ten times the average length of the rest) and it is the most formal and elaborate in concept.

The Bible was a central dynamic in my home when I was growing up and, during my formative years, I began to underline and memorise many of the verses that endeared themselves to my heart – a practice I have continued to this day. I was intrigued when I came to write about this psalm to see how many of its wonderful phrases and texts I had committed to memory.

The outstanding message of this psalm is to encourage us to take God's Word into our hearts and become acquainted with its highways and byways. As a teenager I played the piano at the Bible class that my father led. For the many years I participated in that weekly programme we engaged in something called the 'Bible searcher'. This involved looking for a given verse then the first person to find it standing up and reading it aloud. By this method I learned my way around the Bible. I got the feeling in those years that the Bible was different from every other book and the love that my father had for it entered into me. In this way many key scriptures came to be lodged in my memory, scriptures that have acted like anchors holding me steady in the storms I have encountered in life.

Psalm 119 has 22 eight-verse sections, each beginning with a successive letter of the Hebrew alphabet, and each verse within the section beginning with the same letter. With 176 verses, it is, in fact, the longest chapter in the Bible. Most of its lines are addressed to God, mingling prayers with professions of devotion to God's Law. Devotion to the Word of God and to the God of the Word is the dominant theme.

The psalmist highlights two aspects of that Word: God's directives for life and God's promises – the one calling for obedience and the other for faith. It is a song of joy and rejoicing in the Word of God which, clearly, was the psalmist's delight. When we consider how he treasured it and yet how little he had of it by comparison with the whole of the Bible that we have now, ought we not to feel ashamed at how cold we often are towards it today?

A book about THE Book

Many commentators attribute this psalm to David. Ten times he declares his love for the commandments or testimonies or Law. He acknowledges his errant ways, the need for discipline with its pain but also its fruits, and his suffering at the hands of those who, disregarding God's Word, subject him to ridicule and shame. It has been said of this psalm: 'He that shall read it considerately, it will either warm him or shame him'. Psalm 119 is a book about the Book and my prayer is that, as you go through it, you will fall ever more deeply in love with God's Word, so that your faith will increase and your relationship with God will be enriched.

Some say that this psalm was written in an age similar to our present time: it was a time of religious scepticism when many doubted the existence of God and people jumped from one religious fad to another. It was a very wicked and sinful period when profanity ran rampant.

What is delightful to see is that the psalmist, in an environment that was so hostile to faith and the things of God, instead of wavering, tightened his grip on the Word of God and never, never let go.

What I would like to do in this chapter is to pinpoint just two of the choicest verses in this wonderful psalm, verses that have made an impact on my own life. The first I want to bring to your attention is verse 105:

Your word is a lamp to my feet and a light for my path.

Someone has come up with a catchy tune for a praise song which incorporates these words and I often find myself singing it to myself. Here is no better way of feeding one's spirit than to sing to oneself the actual words of Scripture.

Long ago I came to realise that God's Word is like a compass directing my life's transactions. I have tried to make it the standard for assessing everything that has to do with my life and to be guided by it in all the choices I make.

Our decisions are greatly influenced by four things: the culture (everybody's doing it), tradition (that is the way it has always been done), rationale (what seems most reasonable), and emotions (how I feel at the moment). These four things are very useful for decision-making in many of life's situations but all are fallible and, as Christians, we have another route that we can take – the infallible guidance of Scripture.

A verse that is key to us at CWR is 2 Timothy 3:16: 'All Scripture is given by inspiration of God, and is profitable for doctrine, for reproof, for correction, for instruction in righteousness … ' (NKJV). In every aspect of our ministry, whether through our publications or our training, we are seeking to help people apply God's Word to their everyday lives and relationships.

Selwyn Hughes says that it was early after God called him to be a preacher that he made the decision to trust in the Bible as the authority for his life. He said to God, 'There are many things I don't understand about it but I take it by faith.' This is a decision that every Christian must face. Let me tell you how, in my early thirties, I came to accept the Bible's authority for myself. I asked God to baptise me with His Spirit and I received a gift of faith that has never left me in all the ups and downs of life since. It was at this time that I came to accept by faith the whole of the Bible as the written Word of God. I simply said to myself, 'I am going to take this book as my final referee in everything.' From that time, the Scriptures took on a new dimension as the Spirit brought them to life for me in a wonderful way, and over the years I have never once doubted the Bible's reliability and authority.

God's Word is spiritual food that will renew your mind and transform your Christian life. This is how the apostle Paul puts it: 'Do not conform any longer to the pattern of this world, but be transformed by the renewing of your mind. Then you will be able to test and approve what God's will is – his good, pleasing and perfect will' (Rom. 12:2)

God speaks through His Word

God speaks to us through many different channels – directly, by His Spirit through His Word, or indirectly, through prophecy, other people or our circumstances. In my experience, He speaks most often and most reliably through His Word. As I read the Bible, the Holy Spirit's 'highlighter pen' brings verses to my attention more intimately and personally than any Bible commentator could.

Let me give you an example. When my daughters were young teenagers, I returned to the workplace, taking up a fairly undemanding job with CWR. However, within a short space of time, as a result of sudden staff changes, I found myself working directly for Selwyn Hughes and was asked to take up new responsibilities in setting up and running a small counselling centre in a nearby town. This would involve my leaving the main team office, where there was a lot of fellowship and support, to work on my own for most of the day. Being a sociable person, the prospect was very unappealing to me and the question I asked in my quiet time that evening was: 'Lord, is this Your will for me?' There, in my regular Bible reading for that day, I found His answer in the words of Jeremiah 15:17: 'I sat alone because your hand was on me.' The Holy Spirit quickened that verse to me in an unmistakable way. There was now no doubt in my mind that this was God's will for my life. However much my feelings were crying out to the contrary, I knew that I did not want to be in any other place than where God's hand was upon me. I made that move and took up those responsibilities and, in an amazing way, God used that period in the counselling centre as a stepping-stone to the ministry that would open up for me at Waverley Abbey House in the future years.

His Word is a lamp and a light: it reveals to us things concerning ourselves and things concerning God that otherwise we would not have known. His Word is a lamp that is kept burning with the oil of the Spirit; it is like the lamp in the Temple sanctuary and the pillar of fire to Israel. The Bible commentator Matthew Henry says, 'It must be not only a light to our eyes, to gratify them, but a light to our feet and to our path, to direct us in the choice of our way in general and in the particular steps we take in that way.'

Ian Fraser recounts the following incident in *What's Special About the Bible?*

She was a shy African woman. When teased by her loud-mouthed neighbour, she was tongue-tied, unable to produce a ready answer to her taunts. The reason for the scorn that was heaped upon her was the authority that the shy woman gave to the Bible.

Not only did she read it regularly but, if any problem or dilemma faced her which she found difficult to cope with, she would go into her hut, turn to passages which she thought might help her, meditate upon them, then emerge to deal with the situation.

Things came to a head when, in front of others, her neighbour took her to task: 'There are all kinds of books in the world which can help us find how to live,' she said, 'yet you turn to just one,

always the same one. Why, tell me why? Why this one book?'
At last, the woman's tongue was loosed and the words came:
'Other books I read,' she said. 'This book reads me.'

A friend of mine who leads a weekly Bible study group in her
home told me about one of the members who is extremely well read
and can quote from Tolstoy, Shakespeare, Milton and many of the
great writers and poets of literary fame. However, she doesn't know
her Bible in the same way and often wavers in her life, making unwise
decisions because she doesn't know God's Word well enough for it to
be a light to her path.

As we read and spend time with God in His Word, not only do we
get to know the Bible better, we get to know the author better too. We
can understand more about His ways and can follow more closely the
path He opens up before us.

Another verse that has been so meaningful to me is verse 11:

I have hidden your word in my heart that I might not sin against
you.

A thing may be hidden in two ways, either by concealing it or
else by cherishing and keeping it. In the parable of the talents (Matt.
25:14–30), the unprofitable servant hid his talent in the ground. But
this verse does not speak of concealing but of cherishing God's Word as
a thing of great price. His Word is a treasure worth laying up or storing.
The Word is hidden not for concealment but for safety and it is to be
hidden in our hearts that it might be ready for use whenever we need
it. If it is only in our heads, our memories may fail us but, if it is in our
hearts, the impression of it will remain in our souls and it will be safe.
Scripture, in speaking of 'the heart', has in mind the deepest part of us,
the part with the strongest influence on the way we live our lives.

As I began to write this section, I recalled a situation where I suspected I might have contravened, unwittingly, a legal requirement concerning some photographs I was about to use. My conscience troubled me until I made a phone call to clarify that this was not the case. With the assurance that permission had been granted, I was able to give my attention fully to what I was writing. Having God's Word hidden in our hearts helps us keep a sensitive conscience.

To hide the Word in our heart is to understand and remember it and to be affected by it. 'Let the word of Christ dwell in you richly,' writes Paul (Col. 3:16). If we store His words, as we would precious things, we have them as treasures to be used as the occasion demands. They are always ready for our use, to protect us from sin and wrongdoing.

'Therefore, get rid of all moral filth and the evil that is so prevalent, and humbly accept *the word planted in you*, which can save you' (James 1:21, my italics). The Word is called 'the sword of the Spirit' (Eph. 6:17) and there is great reassurance in having it ready to ward off temptations. When Christ was tempted by the devil, He was equipped with Scripture to overcome His tempter (Matt. 4:1–11).

His Word hidden in our hearts makes our discussions and conversations with others more gracious: '… out of the overflow of the heart, the mouth speaks' (Matt. 12:34). Because there is rapid intercourse between the heart (or soul) and the tongue, whatever is hidden, good or bad, will be expressed by the tongue.

When I was a teenager I was asked to leave the cookery class. My headmistress said to my mother, 'Jeannette's a darling, but she has an undisciplined tongue.' All my life I have struggled to hold back unwise and ill-considered words and, whilst I am much better than I used to be, I am still apt to blurt out things that are unhelpful. There is tremendous power in words and Scripture warns us about this again and again. The tongue is a small thing but what enormous damage it can do (James 3:1–8). The more there is of God's Word in our hearts, the greater its influence will be on what we say.

How do we hide God's Word in our hearts?

Here I want to draw on the wisdom of Beth Clark, a gifted Bible teacher and a valued member of the Women at Waverley teaching team. She is now in her eighties and women of all ages still delight in 'sitting at her feet' as she opens the Scriptures to a group. Beth often reminds us that there are five significant ways of approaching the Bible. All are important but, although listed fifth, meditation is the greatest of these and the best means of hiding God's Word in our hearts. The five ways are:

- Hearing it read aloud
- Reading it yourself
- Studying it alone or with others
- Memorising verses
- Bible meditation

Hearing

We hear the Word of God read in our church services and on various occasions of Christian fellowship. Sometimes I read the Scriptures aloud to myself in my own quiet time because I find it's good to *hear* the Word at the same time as reading it. Driving the car or doing the ironing it's also good to listen to audiocassette or CD recordings of God's Word. But *hearing* the Word has a wider meaning: 'So then faith comes by hearing, and hearing by the word of God' (Rom. 10:17, NKJV). This kind of hearing does not mean just 'listening' but rather 'hearkening' to it. To hearken means *to hear and obey*. The marvellous thing about receiving the Word of God and obeying it is that it opens the road of faith. Failure to act in obedience robs us of the power of faith.

Paul wrote to Timothy: 'Until I come, devote yourself to the public reading of Scripture, to preaching and to teaching' (1 Tim. 4:13). He instructed Timothy to give attention to reading, and we should accept the same instruction.

Reading the Scriptures

This enables us to get a panoramic view of truth and is one of the greatest aids to our meditation because it enables the Holy Spirit to draw on our memory of what we have stored through reading. Truth must not only be seen in the immediate contextual passage, but also in the context of the whole body of truth in the entire Book. Regular reading provides the greatest deterrent to error.

Develop a systematic method of reading. Read everything in the Scriptures, including Leviticus and the genealogies! Remember that 'all Scripture is God-breathed'. At CWR it is our delight to help people understand and become familiar with the Scriptures and that is why we have a range of Bible devotionals for all ages, as well as regular Bible Discovery weekends. We also have a chronological reading programme, Cover to Cover, which goes through the whole Bible in the order in which events happened, thus giving a wonderful sense of the unfolding story in the Scriptures.

I have read through the whole Bible straight through from Genesis to Revelation and have also used CWR's *Cover to Cover* plan, reading through the Bible 'as it happened' twice. Both ways were challenging and fascinating and certainly required 'stickability', but were so wonderfully satisfying to accomplish. Reading the whole of the Bible gives you a perspective on the Scriptures you could not achieve any other way. If you haven't done it yet, I encourage you to do so soon. Beth's husband, Dennis Clark, had read the complete Bible 85 times when he died aged 61. No wonder he was such an incredible Bible teacher!

Study

Paul also wrote to Timothy, 'Do your best to present yourself to God as one approved, a workman who does not need to be ashamed and who correctly handles the word of truth' (2 Tim. 2:15). Study requires discipline, effort, perseverance and sacrifice – the flesh will fight you!

Give some time to studying the Scripture, either alone or with others. There are many good courses available. Why not consider enrolling on one? Philip Greenslade, who leads our Bible Discovery weekends at Waverley Abbey House, is an excellent Bible teacher. He is also author of CWR's Bible Discovery series of books based on these weekends and he contributes to *Cover to Cover Every Day* our in-depth bimonthly Bible reading notes.

Memorisation

We need to learn by heart God's Word. Memory is a gift God gives to each of us. We are able to remember many things that are important to us, such as telephone numbers, addresses, names, ages, songs we sing, to name a few. We have the ability to remember and the memory, being like a muscle, gets stronger the more it is used. There are many times during the day when we can exercise our memory muscle: waiting in line, eating, washing up, travelling, getting ready for bed, are just are a few of them. A good aid to memory is to write a scripture on a card and carry it around with you so you can pull it out to exercise your memory muscle as you have opportunity. Put cards on your bathroom mirror, prop them up in your kitchen, on your desk. The more intentional about this you are, the easier it will become. By continually repeating and memorising a verse, or a psalm, you will find yourself meditating upon it also.

These four great avenues, when put to proper use, will channel enormous benefit into our meditation in the Word, which is the fifth way to approach the Scriptures.

Meditation

Six times in Psalm 119, the psalmist says he will meditate on the Word of God (Psa. 119:15,23,48,78,97,148). Paul instructed Timothy: 'Meditate upon these things; give yourself entirely to them, that your progress may be evident to all' (1 Tim. 4:15, NKJV).

When God commanded Joshua to lead the nation of Israel, here's what He told him to do: 'Do not let this Book of the Law depart from your mouth; meditate on it day and night, so that you may be careful to do everything written in it. Then you will be prosperous and successful' (Josh. 1:8–9). The Lord directs Joshua to the secret of success – meditation in the Word of God

The word 'meditation' comes from the same word from which we derive 'mastication' or, at a lower level, 'chewing the cud'. It implies careful, unrushed, prayerful and serious thought. You take a verse and read it carefully, allow a phrase to roll around in your mind, continually contemplating, pondering and dwelling upon it, viewing it from every angle, weighing it and considering it carefully. We need to do this, not just once, but over and over again, until we begin to talk to ourselves about it and allow it to penetrate, permeate and saturate our thinking.

By mulling over, musing upon and pondering the Word of God, mingled with prayer, the Holy Spirit conveys truth to our heart. The work of meditation is only complete when the word we have come to comprehend goes down into our innermost being and changes our life. Then and only then can we become a living expression of Jesus Christ – 'Christ in you, the hope of glory'.

Psalm 119 contains many marvellous gems of truth that every

believer can commit to memory. Choose your favourites out of this psalm and begin to feed your spirit through meditation and memorisation. It's *never* too late to start.

Questions for reflection

- How do you regard the Bible? Try to write down a number of words that come immediately to your mind.

- What sense do you have that the Bible is a book different from any other? How is it different? What is its effect upon you? Think about your heart and your behaviour as well as your mind.

- What are the major influences in your decision-making? Try to think of a specific decision you took, and be honest about what led you to your decision.

- How, if at all, does the Bible figure in your decision-making? Try to give an example of how you have used it, or might in future use it, in seeking to come to a decision? If you have had the experience of Scripture guiding you in a decision you made, what were the consequences of that decision?

- What things about you and about Himself has God revealed to you through His Word that otherwise you would not have known? Begin to keep a record of these in a special notebook or in any other way you may prefer.

- With Matthew 12:34 in mind, what things hidden within your heart escape by way of your tongue? What might you do to gain better control in this area?

■ Which of the five ways given by Beth Clark to approach the Bible do you regularly practise? If you have not already done so, determine to adopt one or more of these ways and begin today.

■ Could you honestly say that you are acquainted with all the 'highways and byways' of God's Word? What commitment are you willing to make now to gain a wider and deeper knowledge of the Bible?

■ Which verses from Psalm 119 are your favourites? Write some of them on cards and memorise them. Remember, if they are not used, they are soon forgotten!

Chapter Four

A Song of Protection

Psalms 90 and 91

Beverley Shepherd

'Teach us to number our days aright, that we may gain a heart of wisdom.'

(Psalm 90:12)

I wonder what comes to your mind when you think of 'protection'. We are encouraged to protect ourselves in a variety of ways – to protect our privacy with call screening on our phones; protect our homes with elaborate locks and burglar alarms; and our health with various health-promoting foods and vitamins. Living in Britain we often need protection from the weather – an umbrella and waterproofs for the rain, or sun creams with a high SPF in the hot sun. The dictionary defines protection as 'to shield from danger, injury, change, capture or loss'. There are times when we are more aware of our need for protection than at others. Take a moment to reflect on the things from which you currently feel the need of protection and make a note of them.

We will all have developed protective strategies over the years – some of these are appropriate and others may need to be challenged. We may look to others for protection – parents, husbands, the police and fire brigade – or to our savings or insurance policies. I love the Matthew Henry commentary on Genesis that says that God created woman from man's rib so that she should be next to his heart to be beloved, by his side to be equal with him and under his arm for protection.

We may also have decided on a strategy of self-protection, especially when others have failed to protect us, eg:

- Emotional walls around us to protect ourselves from hurt or rejection
- Activity-packed diaries to protect us from loneliness
- Lies to protect us from blame
- Fantasy and denial to protect us from reality
- Sarcasm or dry humour to protect us from people getting too close

- A critical spirit to protect us from being confronted with our own faults
- A false 'super-spirituality' to protect us from having to get real with God
- Shyness to hide the real 'me'

Take time to reflect on the protective strategies that you adopt, to ask God for His insight and for openness to all that He wants to show you.

A few months ago I was reflecting on the self-protective strategies I adopt in the workplace and wrote the following:

Lord,
Thank You that when You formed me in my mother's womb
You made me a woman.
I'm a woman who works in a man's world – and most days that's fine.
Most days it's fun.

But every now and then … I notice …
I notice the professional shell I have put around myself
I notice the sharp words I use to shield my vulnerability
I notice the desensitising that protects me from hurt
I notice the temptation to hide my femininity –
Especially when others ignore or devalue me as a woman.

Thank You that You see me
Thank You that I am precious and honoured in Your sight
Thank You that Your oil and wine tenderise my toughened skin
And You, O Lord Most High, are all the protection I need.
Thank You that You see and celebrate Your creation – Your woman
– me!

Today, as I work, help me to remember and enjoy
The woman You created me to be.
Amen.[1]

When I came to study Psalm 90 I realised that those things from which I considered myself in most need of protection (refer to your own list that you made) were not things that God was saying I should fear – my greatest fear should be of His anger! God's anger is not a popular subject – in a pendulum swing away from the fire and brimstone preaching of a century ago we emphasise God's love to the exclusion of His wrath. The Bible, and in particular Psalm 90, does not have this bias.

Our need of protection

This psalm explores seven areas in which we are in need of God's protection:

1. God's anger

In verse 7 we read, 'We are consumed by your anger and terrified by your indignation' and in verse 11: 'Who knows the power of your anger? For your wrath is as great as the fear that is due to you.' This psalm takes God's anger seriously. In reading through Leviticus, Numbers and Deuteronomy recently, I have been struck again and again by the holiness of our God, a holiness that is emphasised by the penalty for defiling His holy day, the Sabbath, His holy tabernacle, His holy laws and His holy name – death. When we fail to respect God's holiness and His anger, it is all too easy to trivialise our own sin and to disregard the command to be holy. To be a holy people means to be 'set apart'. 'I am the LORD your God, who has set you apart from the nations' (Lev. 20:24). We are meant to be distinctive in the way we live. This is emphasised in the New Testament by Jesus:

I tell you, my friends, do not be afraid of those who kill the body and after that can do no more. But I will show you whom you should fear: Fear him who, after the killing of the body, has power to throw you into hell. Yes, I tell you, fear him.'
(Luke 12:4–5)

2. Futility

Have you ever wondered if your life has any point? You clean the house and it soon gets messed up again; you write a report that no one bothers to read; you put in a new business proposal knowing that your manager is not open to change; or you discipline your children wondering if their behaviour will ever change. It is a question that has perplexed scholars and philosophers down the ages. The writer of Ecclesiastes, generally thought to be Solomon (the wisest man of his time), set himself the goal of studying and personally experiencing everything that could possibly give his life meaning – pleasure, work, achievement, riches, etc and came to the following conclusion: '"Meaningless! Meaningless!" says the Teacher. "Utterly meaningless! Everything is meaningless"' (Eccl. 1:2). Why does he come to this conclusion? Because of death.

Psalm 90 picks up on this theme: 'You sweep men away in the sleep of death; they are like the new grass of the morning – though in the morning it springs up new, by evening it is dry and withered' (vv.5–6), and 'The length of our days is seventy years – or eighty, if we have the strength; yet their span is but trouble and sorrow, for they quickly pass, and we fly away' (v.10).

3. Ourselves

Yes, we need protection from our own sinful nature. 'You have set our iniquities before you, our secret sins in the light of your presence' (Psa. 90:8). Why do we sin? Because we want to and because temptation is tempting …

Many years ago *The Times* newspaper published an exchange of correspondence concerning the nature of evil and the problem with the world. A short letter from G.K. Chesterton was included:

> Dear Sirs
> You ask what is wrong with humanity.
> I am.
> Yours sincerely
> G.K. Chesterton

4. Illness

We live in a fallen world and our bodies are mortal – hence we get sick and die. Together with the whole of creation, we groan as we eagerly await our adoption as sons and the redemption of our bodies (Rom. 8:22–23). Yet we are encouraged in Psalm 91 to ask for God's protection in this area: '… the pestilence that stalks in the darkness …' (v.6).

5. Worry

Have you ever lain awake at night worrying? I believe that 'the terror of the night' (Psa. 91:5) could refer to all those concerns that crowd in on us in those sleepless hours. Caution and worry are different. Caution leads to appropriate preparation whereas worry leads to mental paralysis. I'm told that the command 'Do not worry' occurs 366 times in the Bible. I've never counted them but, if true, this means that there is a 'Do not worry' for every day of the year including leap years! Worry about tomorrow can prevent us living in the fullness of God's provision for today.

6. Our enemies

Unfortunately we all have people in our lives that act or speak against us. The term 'enemies' may seem harsh and yet that is what their actions or words make them. Psalm 91 is instructive in the illustrations it uses. The fowler's snare (v.3) – are there people who are deliberately trying to trap you? A manager in a Christian organisation told me of an email sent by a colleague whom she considered a friend. The email suggested she investigate a particular matter and copied in several senior managers. That colleague knew that she had already investigated the matter fully and his email was merely an attempt to score points. The arrow that flies by day (v.5) – the lyrics of a song once heard come to mind: 'I have broken bones, not from sticks and stones. It was the words that hurt me.' Words have real power to wound. The lion (v.13) denotes the obvious open assault. Predatory animals often pick off the weakest in a group to attack or those who have allowed themselves to become isolated. In the Bible the cobra and the serpent (v.13) are often representative of the devil and his schemes. Instead of the open attack he sows doubt in God's character and His Word. As with Eve in Genesis 3:1–5 the devil's strategy is to question God's motives and commands: 'Did God really say …?'; 'You will not surely die …'

7. The devil

I had the joy of seeing with a good friend a Mystery play, staged at a London theatre. Typically Mystery plays tell God's story from creation through to resurrection and this one was no exception. What struck me was the presence of the devil (clad in a vivid red leather outfit) in every scene – he was the serpent in the garden, he tried to prevent the removal of the stone covering Lazarus's tomb, he held the basin for Pilate as he washed his hands, and crowed three times in Peter's hearing. Yet we, as Christians, can be woefully unaware of the spiritual battle around us. In Ephesians, Paul reminds us of the devil's schemes and the spiritual forces of evil (Eph. 6:11–12). It's a warning we need to take seriously.

The source of our protection

If Psalm 90 highlights our need of protection, then Psalm 91 emphasises the source of our protection. Clearly in this psalm it is God Himself who is our protection – through His character, His propitiation, His salvation, His favour and His presence.

1. God's character

Psalm 91 tells us that our God is the 'Most High', 'Almighty', 'LORD', 'my God' and 'faithful'. Our real protection comes from the very character of our heavenly Father.

Two famous botanists were once touring in the glens of Scotland in search of rare specimens to add to their collections, when one of them spotted a quite remarkable flower. The difficulty was that it was growing down a deep gully, too narrow for them to access as grown men. In the local village they found a lad who they thought might be willing to be lowered down on a rope and pick the flower for them. They offered him increasing sums of money but with each offer he refused. Eventually they asked him what would persuade him to go down the gulley for them. He replied 'I'll only do it if my father is holding the end of the rope.' He knew his father wouldn't let him fall. Neither will our heavenly Father let us fall.[2]

2. God's propitiation

Propitiation means the removal of wrath by the offering of a gift or appropriate sacrifice.

One Sunday, on a cycling holiday with a friend of mine, we stopped at a church en route for the morning service. The preacher began his sermon with a rejection of the whole idea of an angry God, and went on to reject the death of Christ as a propitiation for our sins. Both my friend and I reacted strongly to this denial of what God says about Himself in the Bible. I put my head down and prayed that no one would listen to him – my friend was braver: she stood up, mid-sermon, with tears pouring down her face and told the congregation that this preacher was lying to them and not to listen to him. We are not free to define who God is – He has told us clearly about Himself, His anger, and His mercy as the following verses testify:

> Yet he was merciful;
> > he forgave their iniquities
> > and did not destroy them.
> Time after time he restrained his anger
> > and did not stir up his full wrath.
> > > (Psa. 78:38)

> Surely he took up our infirmities
> > and carried our sorrows,
> yet we considered him stricken by God,
> > smitten by him, and afflicted.
> But he was pierced for our transgressions,
> > he was crushed for our iniquities;
> the punishment that brought us peace was upon him,
> > and by his wounds we are healed.
> > > (Isa. 53:4–5)

> [Jesus Christ] Himself is the propitiation for our sins ...
> > (1 John 2:2, NKJV)

Kiss the Son, lest he be angry
and you be destroyed in your way ...
(Psa. 2:12)

Where do we flee from God's wrath? To God Himself!

3. God's salvation

As a child I was a great fan of *Thunderbirds*. For those not in the
know, *Thunderbirds* is the story of the Tracey family, who live on an
idyllic desert island and who are summoned into action with a call
for help to 'International Rescue'. Their response is immediate, the
swimming pool rolls back revealing the launch pad for the various
Thunderbird aircraft and within minutes 'Thunderbirds are go!'
– speeding their way to effect the most amazing rescue.

Exciting as International Rescue is, it doesn't begin to touch on
God's response when we cry out to Him. I challenge you to read
through Psalm 18:3–19 and not be stirred – He doesn't just roll back
the pool, He parts the heavens; He doesn't send aircraft, but hailstones
and bolts of lightning; He reaches down from on high and takes hold
of us!

Psalm 91 emphasises His salvation again and again: 'he saves', 'he
covers', 'he commands his angels', 'he guards', 'he rescues', 'he protects',
'he answers', and 'he delivers'. Why – because He delights in us (Psa.
18:19)!

4. God's favour

Earlier in this chapter we looked at how our life may seem without
purpose or meaning. God answers the futility of our lives with His
favour. The psalmist asks God to 'Satisfy us in the morning with
your unfailing love ...' (Psa. 90:14) and 'May the favour of the Lord

our God rest upon us; establish the work of our hands for us – yes, establish the work of our hands' (Psa. 90:17). God can permeate everything we do, say and are with meaning and purpose – a purpose that will last beyond death if we are willing to allow Him to direct us. The story of the captive servant girl in 2 Kings 5 illustrates how God can use each of our lives. She has been captured, taken away from home and family and made to work for Naaman's wife as a servant. If she had had hopes and plans for her life they had come to nothing. Yet it is here in this captive situation that God established the work of her hands. She obviously serves her master and mistress well and cares for them – enough to risk speaking out and suggesting that Naaman seek a cure for his leprosy from Elisha, God's prophet. God gave her life purpose and her story has brought encouragement and challenge to millions down the centuries.

5. God's presence

God's presence is our protection. '… I will be with him in trouble …' (Psa. 91:15). A very real example of this is given by an American missionary who worked in a field hospital in Africa. While home on leave he shared the following story with his church. Every fortnight he made a two-day bicycle journey through the jungle to a town to buy medical supplies. This meant spending one night in the jungle. One day when he came to the town he saw two men fighting. As one of them was injured, he treated him before buying the supplies. A fortnight later when he was again in the town the young man approached him and told of how he and some friends had followed him into the jungle on his last visit. 'We were about to kill you when we saw you were surrounded by twenty-six armed guards. All five of my friends saw them. We were afraid and left you alone.' At this point in his talk, the missionary was interrupted by a member of the congregation wanting to check when the incident occurred.

When told the date, the man took over the story. 'On the night of the incident in Africa it was morning here, and I was preparing to go and play golf. I was about to putt when I felt a strong urge to pray for you. In fact I couldn't continue the game, and I called some men to meet me in the sanctuary and to pray for you.' He then asked the men who had met to pray to stand – there were twenty-six![3]

'Never will I leave you;
never will I forsake you.'
So we say with confidence,
'The Lord is my helper; I will not be afraid.
    What can man do to me?'

(Heb. 13:6)

How do we access God's protection – what is our part?

In a fascinating TV programme some while ago two ex-burglars were giving advice to a couple on how to protect their home. One of their comments intrigued me – that most people with a burglar alarm did not bother to use it! Often people were too lazy to switch it on or didn't want it to go off accidentally. We can be like that with God's protection – we can fail to access it. Psalms 90 and 91 are clear as to how we place ourselves under God's protection: we are to fear Him; to number our days aright; to dwell; to rest; to trust; to tell others; to love Him; to acknowledge God's name; and to call on Him. Let me encourage you, through these two psalms, to recognise your need of protection and to trust God as your protector.

But you are a shield around me, O LORD,
    you bestow glory on me and lift up my head.

(Psa. 3:3)

Questions for reflection

- From what are you currently in need of protection?

- What self-protection strategies are you aware of?

- Use these two psalms to reflect on both God's anger and His great compassion and mercy.

- Who can you join with to pray protection for your own lives, your family, your church and for missionaries?

- Note down examples from your own experience of God's protection.

Notes

1. Originally published in *Pocket Prayers for Work*, compiled by Mark Greene (Church House Publishing, 2004).

2. Adapted from *A Dose of Salts* by Simon Coupland, (Monarch Publications, 1997), from an illustration used by Daniel Cozens in Cambridge, 1982.

3. Jane Holloway, *Prayer for Amateurs* (Hodder and Stoughton, 2000).

Chapter Five

A Song of Two Ways

Psalm 73

Jeannette Barwick

'"For my thoughts are not your thoughts,
neither are your ways my ways," declares the Lord.'

(Isaiah 55:8)

The 73rd Psalm may not be as well known as the 23rd Psalm but I think it deserves to be, for the truths and insights it contains provide us with one of the most steadying and encouraging revelations to be found anywhere in the Word of God.

It is attributed to Asaph, a priest appointed by King David. The issue with which he is struggling is this: why should the godly suffer so much when the ungodly, generally speaking, seem to get off scot-free? So deeply does this question cut into his soul that he is brought to the point of near despair: '… my feet had almost slipped; I had nearly lost my foothold' (v.2).

This is also one of the most emotionally intense psalms. Asaph confesses to feeling envious of the prosperity of the ungodly. His very remarkable honesty is the hallmark of many of the psalmists. In telling us the truth about himself, Asaph shows the contrast between him and God and he ministers to the glory of God.

Selwyn Hughes, whose insights on this psalm I have drawn upon,[1] says,

Are you puzzled by the fact that, though you are following the Lord, life is extremely difficult? Do you wonder why those who live in opposition to the Almighty seem to have an easier time than those who are committed to His cause? Asaph found a foothold on this slippery path of doubt and so can we.

In his struggles, Asaph discovers some spiritual principles that radically alter his perspectives and bring him step by step to the heights of confident spiritual assurance. Together, we too are now going to discover a few more footholds for our faith.

Surely God is good (v.1)

Asaph begins on a note of great triumph: '*Surely God is good to Israel, to those who are pure in heart*'. Preachers usually leave their conclusion until the end of their talk or sermon – but here he begins with it! The reason is that he is so convinced of the fact that God is good that he decides to start right there. It is as if he is saying, 'I want to tell you how I moved from doubt to faith, but the thing I want you to get right away is this: *God is good.*'

Some commentators believe that, in the Temple services, there was a time of open testimony and worship, similar to the old Methodist class meetings when individuals gave testimonies to their fellow believers of God's dealings with them. This is one of the most powerful ways of building up the spiritual life of the Church. Imagine the impact Asaph's story would have made upon his listeners as he related how he had emerged from the experience of crippling doubt to renewed confidence in the goodness of God.

Every one of us will know something of the problem with which the psalmist struggled. We start off with a positive faith in the goodness of God and then something happens which causes us to be plagued with doubts. The problem then is how to get back to where we were. In this psalm Asaph is at pains to show us how to arrive back at the place where the soul finds its true peace.

I am always encouraged by remembering that the strongest convictions are often born out of the throes of doubt and discouragement. The statement 'God is good to Israel' is not a mere cliché; it is a statement grounded in experience.

Wrong comparisons (vv.1–3)

Asaph tells us what caused him to move away from that belief so that his soul became filled with such desolating doubt that his feet almost slipped. Slowly the unfairness of everything he could see around him – the prosperity of wicked people who lived their lives for themselves and reaped all the benefits – had begun to wear him down. He was filled with envy and his faith was shaken.

How commendable is his honesty! How many of us, I wonder, myself included, are as honest as the writer of this impressive psalm? Sometimes, I think, we pretend that things are not affecting us as much as they really are. We deny or ignore our true feelings, which is in fact spiritually damaging.

Asaph doesn't hesitate to tell the truth about himself. He brings home to us the importance of acknowledging what is going on in our hearts when we are caught up in the midst of struggle and conflict. Some Christian teachers maintain that we should never allow any negative thoughts or feelings and should always live life positively. At CWR we are all in favour of taking a positive approach to life but how can you achieve this until you have clearly identified what is troubling you? Once an issue has been faced, and faced realistically, then it can and must be dealt with in a positive way.

Actually, it can be very discouraging to meet the kind of person who always gives the impression that he or she is walking on the mountain top. Those who have the grace and honesty to admit to struggles and failures are usually more helpful to us. Spiritual growth begins when we realistically and honestly face up to the struggles that are going on inside us.

Asaph took his eyes off the Lord for a while and began to compare himself and his circumstances with those of the wicked. Soon envy soured his heart.

What exactly is envy? It is malicious grudging, a wanting to gain what we do not have. One psychologist concludes that it is born of a deep love of self: someone has something we want and we will not be content until we have it.

The late Dr William Sangster (an esteemed English Methodist preacher) wrote:

To practise comparison with one's fellows is often to be trapped into sin. If we are not as virtuous as they are, we are tempted to imply that it is only in appearance and they are possibly hypocrites; if they have tasted more of the sweetness of success than we have done, we often slide into envy.

The road to sin (vv.4–12)

Asaph describes the apparently carefree and successful life of the godless people around him: 'They have no struggles; their bodies are healthy and strong. They are free from the burdens common to man; they are not plagued by human ills' (v.4). They seemed to have the least share of the troubles and calamities of this life, causing him to conclude: 'This is what the wicked are like – always carefree, they increase in wealth' (v.12).

Envy distorts reality. It exaggerates situations and becomes more engrossed in generalities than specifics. Asaph had compared his lack to the abundance of others (perhaps only a few people) until the comparison had occupied his whole mind and distorted his thinking. Envy had seeped into his soul and made others appear happier and better off than they really were. And this comparison had a negative effect upon him personally as he considered himself as being worse off and poorer than in fact he was.

It's easy to find ourselves sharing Asaph's fascination with the prosperity of the ungodly. Wealth is a favourite topic of conversation and quite frequently we read in our newspapers about the Top Ten, or the Top Hundred, Wealthiest People. But wealth alone can't ensure happiness, although that is what society's attitude towards money seems to indicate. Take stock of where *your* values lie.

Someone told me the other day about a conversation she had had with other Christian friends who all agreed that Christians seemed not to attach as much importance to envy as a sin as to some of the other feelings and thoughts that are considered actually or potentially sinful. Our culture gives us every encouragement to envy and covet others' possessions and positions these days, especially through advertising which presses our buttons with great skill. 'She has such and such – why shouldn't I?'

Envy was the focus of a recent article in a UK Sunday newspaper magazine, illustrated by a green-eyed woman and entitled 'I Want What She's Got'. We're better off than we have ever been, the article claimed, and yet we spend our lives focusing on what we haven't got. Challengingly, the writer asked her readers why we're so consumed with envy. It's a question I would put to you.

Because envy is a sin that can lead to further sin we must carefully watch our tendency to compare ourselves with others, especially those who are apparently more fortunate than we are. We see around us those who seem to be healthier, more successful at work or in other situations, better at building relationships, with more and better worldly possessions than we have. In each of us there is a weakness or a susceptibility that may cause envy to rise up in our hearts. Sometimes it is not the material advantages of others that 'get' to us but relational things like a close friendship, or a happy marriage, or having children.

When we approach life with a grudge born of wrong comparisons we have a distorted picture of the world. The arrogant (the psalmist's word for those who revel in their riches and think only of themselves) may look as if they have everything. The truth, however, is that things that are material, worldly or temporal do not ultimately satisfy. The way of righteousness is sometimes not easy, but it is foolish to compare it with the life of those who seem to have everything – and yet have nothing. They have power but no peace, riches but no inner rest. We read of the lives of the rich and famous every day and their desperate search for happiness which often leads to drugs, drink, illicit affairs, business swindles.

The heart of the issue (vv.11–14)

Now we come to the heart of the issue with which Asaph is grappling. He has hinted at it before but now it comes right out into the open: 'Surely in vain have I kept my heart pure; in vain have I washed my hands in innocence. All day long I have been plagued; I have been punished every morning.'

The Message by Eugene Peterson paraphrases verses 11–14 like this:

> What's going on here? Is God out to lunch?
>> Nobody's tending the store.
> The wicked get by with everything,
>> they have it made, piling up riches.
> I've been stupid to play by the rules;
>> what has it gotten me?
> A long run of bad luck, that's what –
>> a slap in the face every time I walk out the door.

The problem, then, is not so much the prosperity of the wicked as the fact that Asaph himself is passing through a period of great trial and difficulty while they are getting off scot-free. In addition to envy, he was grappling with another feeling – the futility of remaining pure. He had done his best to obey the Law and lead a godly life, but this did not seem to have brought him any benefits.

Perhaps at this point thoughts such as these were running through his mind: 'What's the point of remaining pure since it is the wicked who get all the blessings of life while the righteous have to be content with the dregs? Why can't God take care of His own in the same way that the devil seems to take care of his own?'

The emotion of envy was a symptom of the disease in his soul: the suspicion that God is not good. This brings us to the real root of Asaph's sin: doubt about the goodness of God. Embedded like splintered glass at the core of our souls is the suspicion that God does not have our best interests at heart. Unless that issue is exposed and dealt with, our hearts will never be truly pure. Asaph overcame his suspicions about God's goodness only after envy had exposed what lay in his heart.

Envy is born not only of wrong comparisons but also of ignorance. Ignorance gives rise to envy because, very often, our judgments of people are based only on what we see, and we fail to take account of other things that may be going on in their lives. If we could see beneath the surface – the hidden hurts, the emptiness, the repressed conflicts, the heartaches, the pain, the remorse, the guilt and the fears – then I doubt whether the emotion of envy would ever rise within us.

The turning point (vv.15–16)

In verses 15–16 the psalmist takes the first step towards the resolution of his problem: 'If I had said, "I will speak thus," I would have betrayed your children. When I tried to understand all this, it was oppressive to me …' We see in these words what it was that arrested his feelings of doubt and despair: the thought that if he were to speak out of his discouraged heart he would put a stumbling-block in someone else's path. 'If I did that,' he thinks to himself, 'I would be untrue to the generation of God's children so, rather than discourage others with my doubts, I will not say anything at all.'

What stopped Asaph's spiritual slide was something very simple and ordinary: he made a decision not to say what was on the tip of his tongue. Rather than spread his unbelief, he determined to keep his mouth shut. It might not have been a particularly high spiritual motive, but it was the thing that prevented him from falling. By simply *not* saying something, he prevented himself from falling.

Though filled with doubts about the goodness of God, he nevertheless refrained from expressing those doubts to others. He carefully considered what effect his action might have on the family of God. By changing his focus and thinking of others he stopped himself sliding.

Scripture warns us again and again about the awesome power of words:

> The tongue has the power of life and death ... (Prov. 18:21)
> The tongue is a small thing but what enormous damage it can do.
> A great forest can be set on fire by one tiny spark ... (James 3:5)

Let's think about the words we would like to take back. I would give a great deal to take back some of the things I have said to people over the years. Asaph carefully considered what effect his words might have had on the family of God and kept silent. There is a saying: 'Silence is golden', and in many situations it is. Although he had stopped sliding, Asaph was still in great pain and anguish. 'When I tried to understand all this, it was oppressive to me' (v.16). *The Message* puts it this way: 'When I tried to figure it out all I got was a splitting headache.' I know the feeling!

The power of a new perspective (v.17)

Asaph's thoughts and perplexities concerning the prosperity of the ungodly were finally resolved, not by grabbing at superficial answers, but by going into the sanctuary of God. Here his entire perspective changed and he could begin to see the whole situation from God's point of view. He had tried to figure it out himself but then he entered the sanctuary of God and finally understood the ultimate destiny of the wicked. As *The Message* puts it: '... Until I entered the sanctuary of God, then I saw the whole picture.' Having first considered the consequences of his actions on his brethren, his next step was to go and meet with them in the sanctuary.

Meeting together in Christian fellowship can bring about a radical change in our perspective something that can happen to us when we are alone, of course, but the chances are it will happen more swiftly in the act of corporate worship. Prior to this, had Asaph, like so many whose hearts are filled with envy and uncertainty, stayed away from the place of worship? I wonder what changed his perspective after entering the sanctuary. Was it the singing of one of the psalms, or the prayers of the faithful? We will never know, but one thing is sure: his thinking was changed from natural thinking to spiritual thinking. He had been reasoning like a natural man, considering life from just one viewpoint but, in the sanctuary, he started to look beyond the present to the future.

Many years ago I experienced the great sadness of a broken marriage. At the time I was in a great deal of pain and anguish and I did find the comfort of God in 'the sanctuary'. In church on a Sunday morning, although often moist-eyed and reluctant to talk to anyone about my situation, I would draw strength from being in the company of God's people, singing hymns and hearing the Word of God read and preached. I lived a few miles from the Methodist church where I had worshipped since childhood so, during the week, the local Anglican vicar welcomed me to the mid-week communion service at the parish church where I gratefully partook of the 'means of grace' in the company of other believers. And so I knew God's strengthening and comfort in my sorrow. Being in 'the sanctuary' helped me to find God's perspective on my life, giving me hope beyond my difficulties.

What is the difference between natural and spiritual thinking? Natural thinking is on the level of this world, spiritual thinking is on the level of God. Though Asaph was a good and godly man, he had reverted, under the pressure of circumstances, to thinking 'naturally' about his problem. In the sanctuary, however, he came to understand the final destiny of the wicked. When he saw this, everything came into focus. He had looked at the prosperity of the wicked but he had not considered their end. When he realised the final destiny of the unrepentant wicked – eternity in hell – his thinking was transformed. Better temporary privation than eternal damnation.

The key to a changed perspective always lies in our understanding, the renewing of our minds spoken of in Roman 12:2. In the presence of God the psalmist was given clear judgment. This is an extremely important point which cannot be emphasised too often. What he found in the sanctuary was far more than a pleasant spiritual feeling; he gained a new spiritual consciousness. He was put right in his thinking. He did not merely forget his problem for a while; he found the solution.

The idea many believers have concerning the house of God is that it is a good place to go in order to forget one's troubles for a while. They are soothed by the music and the singing or, in some churches, by the beauty of the architecture. If the practice of our faith does nothing more than excite our emotions and fails to give us a clearer spiritual understanding, then we need to take stock of ourselves. We are lop-sided Christians. The message of Scripture is addressed mainly to our understanding. It does not only teach us about spiritual experience; it enables us to understand life.

In the sanctuary the psalmist found an explanation for the way he felt. He was not given respite that would last merely for a few days; he was given a solution that would stay with him for the rest of his life. It was this, in fact, that caused him to write the psalm we are focusing on at present. He had been seeing things partially and incompletely but now, in the sanctuary, he began to see the whole picture. He gained a proper perspective. Much of the inner turmoil we go through is because we do not see life as a whole and do not consider the bigger picture.

Prejudice has been defined as 'seeing only what you want to see'. People who are prejudiced insist: 'But I have always seen it that way.' Precisely! That's their problem. Their eyes are focused on just one aspect of an issue and they will not allow themselves to look at other aspects. Natural thinking is partial and incomplete. The only way you can see life whole is to stand in the presence of God, read His Word and think His thoughts after Him. And being in fellowship with others in the sanctuary of the church can change our natural thinking.

How foolish we are when we look enviously at the lifestyle of the ungodly, focusing only on their present successes and the marvellous time they seem to be having, without considering their end. In the sanctuary Asaph was reminded of something he had forgotten – the final destiny of the wicked. And when his thinking was changed, his feelings were changed also.

Where does it all end? (vv.18–20)

But there is another insight that he gained in the sanctuary: 'Surely you place them on slippery ground; you cast them down to ruin' (v.18). Why does God do this? In order that He might demonstrate how unreliable and insecure are the ways of those who choose not to walk with Him. This explains why so frequently we read of some celebrity or multi-millionaire coming to grief and losing his or her celebrity status or riches. God often makes a spectacle of those who persist in rejecting His love and grace. Their feet are placed on 'slippery ground'. Remember that when you read your daily newspaper and follow what is happening in the world.

' "For my thoughts are not your thoughts, neither are your ways my ways," declares the LORD' (Isa. 55:8). Whatever we might think about the ways of God, these words give us the ultimate answer: the Almighty acts in ways that are above and beyond our comprehension.

It's as if God is saying, 'When you look at My ways you must not approach them on a natural level, because if you do you will be baffled and overwhelmed. I act on a higher level than the natural, and if you want to understand Me, then you must come up on this level too.' The more we learn to think spiritually about life's problems, the less perplexed we will be.

As Asaph considered the final destiny of the ungodly, everything came into focus for him. He had looked at the prosperity of the ungodly but he had not looked at their end, he had not taken in all the facts. We ought never to forget that it is not how things are at present that is important; it's how they end that matters.

An inside look (vv.21–22)

Asaph was not only put right in his thinking about the ungodly and about God, he was also put right about himself. 'When I was beleaguered and bitter, totally consumed by envy, I was totally ignorant, a dumb ox in your very presence' (*The Message*). Outside the sanctuary, he felt full of self-pity; inside the sanctuary, he had an entirely different view of himself.

Self-pity (and, for that matter, the pity of others) acts like an anodyne: it stops us moving on; it is a humanistic way of dealing with our pain but it does nothing for us spiritually. We say to ourselves, 'There, there. Of course I'm justified in feeling like this', and we can get stuck. We have to be ruthless with ourselves when we are dealing with self-pity. All through my recovery from my broken marriage, I had to determine again and again not to slide into self-pity.

Inside the sanctuary the psalmist had an entirely different view of himself. This is the moment when he faced himself honestly, something that can be difficult to do. He examined himself in the presence of God and discovered there the things that had led him astray.

Always with Him (vv.23–26)

The self-examination brought him to a place of utter abandonment before God and his heart was flooded with instant reassurance: 'Yet I am always with you …' (v.23). He looked into the face of his heavenly Father and realised that he was accepted and loved. The inevitable consequence of working through our problems in the presence of God is that we worship Him.

Asaph proclaims, 'My flesh and my heart may fail, but God is the strength of my heart and my portion for ever' (v.26). Learn this by heart now and keep meditating on these words of life in the days to come.

A song of two ways (vv.27–28)

When it comes down to it, there are only two positions in life – close to God or far away from Him. The psalmist resolved to draw near to God and stay near to Him: 'But as for me, it is good to be near God. I have made the Sovereign LORD my refuge …' (v.28). Let's make this our resolution too.

Questions for reflection

■ What event or events in your life have caused you to question God's goodness?

■ To whom do you compare yourself and your situation and what is the effect of making such comparisons?

■ What, if anything, do you envy in others?

■ Are you generally aware of the possible effect upon others of your words and therefore careful in what you say about your thoughts and feelings? To whom have you spoken words that you would like to take back? You might like to write down a prayer that expresses your feelings about this, now.

■ Where do you go for comfort and help in times of pain and anguish?

■ What 'natural thinking' of yours needs to change?

■ Try to summarise the new perspective you have gained from studying Asaph's psalm. How have you learned to think differently about yourself, your situation and about God?

Notes
1. Selwyn Hughes, 'The Power of a New Perspective', *Every Day with Jesus*, July/August 1989.

Chapter Six

A Song of Thankfulness

Psalm 103

Beverley Shepherd

'Praise the Lord, O my soul;
and forget not all his benefits.'

(Psalm 103:2)

God's blessings

As I sit here in front of my computer in a room overlooking the River Thames it is easy to praise God for all His benefits, yet David commands his soul to praise the Lord irrespective of circumstances. No matter how difficult things are we have a choice to praise Him or not to praise Him, to thank Him or not. We are not to wait until we feel like it to praise God – rather, by using our will and our mind and our memory we can focus on reasons to praise and so kindle our emotions.

This was forcibly brought home to me in reading the testimony of a Chinese pastor who spent 18 years in prison for his faith:

> My friends wonder what kind of work I did in the labour camp to keep me physically healthy. I answered them that life in the labour camp was very, very, very hard. The authorities put me to emptying the human waste cesspool. But they did not know in those years how much I enjoyed working there.
>
> It was more than two metres in breadth and two metres in length, filled with human waste collected from the entire camp. Because the pit was so deep, I could not reach the bottom to empty it, so I had to walk into the disease-ridden mass, and scoop out successive layers of waste, all the time breathing the strong stench. The guards and all the prisoners kept a long way off because of the smell.
>
> So why did I enjoy working in the cesspool? In the labour camp all the prisoners were normally under strict surveillance and no one could be alone. But when I worked in the cesspool I could be alone and could pray to our Lord as I needed. I could recite the Scriptures including all the Psalms I still remembered, and no one was close enough to protest. That's the reason I enjoyed working in the cesspool. Also I could sing loudly all the hymns

I still remembered ... He never left me or forsook me. And so I survived, and the cesspool became my private garden.[1]

Psalm 103 gives us numerous reasons to praise God:

He forgives my sins
He heals my diseases
He redeems my life from the pit
He crowns me with love and compassion
He satisfies my desires with good things
He renews my energy and vigour

He forgives my sins

The woman in Luke 7:37–38 knew what it was like to have her many sins forgiven and her response is extravagant worship. She wets Jesus' feet with her tears and dries them with her hair, kissing them and pouring perfume on them. This is the praise of someone who knows herself to be forgiven and washed clean inside. Meanwhile Simon the Pharisee looks on disdainfully – although just as much a sinner as the woman, he has failed to recognise his need of forgiveness and had not offered Jesus even the common courtesies of a guest in his home. When I view my sin lightly I can, like Simon, fail to recognise my need for forgiveness and so fail to offer Jesus the thankfulness He merits.

He crowns me with love and compassion

Crowns are visible and when we know ourselves to be loved it shows. I remember hearing the story of a newly-engaged couple visiting the vicar to talk about getting married. The vicar was an older man and while he conducted the marriage interview his wife sat quietly nearby doing her embroidery. The young couple sat so close to each other that you could not have got a postcard between them and the groom-to-be thought it must be evident to all how much in love they were. At one point the vicar turned to his wife and she looked up at him and smiled – the look contained such a wealth and depth of love that the young man knew he still had a lot to learn about love! Jesus looks at us in that way – we are the apple of His eye.

He satisfies my desires with good things

Just as I need to train my physical appetite to desire good food and not just sweets, biscuits or chocolate, so God trains our inner desires to want what is good. It is these desires He satisfies.

He renews my energy and vigour

When the psalmist says that God restores our youth he is not talking about a total make-over and face lift, though many of us would not be adverse to that! No the example of Caleb is much more relevant here. Caleb was one of the 12 spies who went into Canaan to bring back a report to Moses and the Israelites before they entered the land. Joshua and Caleb trusted that God could give them victory despite the giants and fortified cities, yet the people chose to listen to the pessimistic reports from the other ten spies and they died in the wilderness as a result. When the surviving Israelites did eventually enter the land 45 years later, Caleb declares: 'Now then, just as the LORD promised, he has kept me alive for forty-five years since the time he said this to Moses, while Israel moved about in the desert. So here I am today, eight-five years old! I am still as strong today as the day Moses sent me out; I am just as vigorous to go out to battle now as I was then. Now give me this hill country that the LORD promised me that day'

(Josh. 14:10–12). Oh to be a Caleb and to be positive and enthusiastic about all the Lord has called me to whatever my age!

Why thank God?

God doesn't need our thanks but we need to say thank you. Thankfulness to God changes us in a variety of ways. It reminds us that we are dependent on Him for our life, health, the food we eat … and so helps counter any temptation to pride.

Thanking God for past blessings and current situations opens us up to receive what He is doing and gives us expectancy for the future. When the barren woman of Isaiah 54 (Zion) is commanded to sing she is still barren – she is not to await pregnancy before opening her mouth. Praise changes the situation because through it we declare our belief that God is in control. Anything other than praise attributes more power to people or to circumstances than to God.

Yet we are also to thank and praise God in adverse circumstances: 'Though the fig-tree does not bud and there are no grapes on the vines, though the olive crop fails and the fields produce no food … yet I will rejoice in the LORD, I will be joyful in God my Saviour' (Hab. 3:17–18). In doing so we are giving up our desire to understand everything and our perceived right to blessings. Instead we are declaring our trust in God's sovereignty and love.

Thankfulness and praise are keys to answered prayer; there is a wonderful example of this in 2 Chronicles 20:

> After consulting the people, Jehoshaphat appointed men to sing to the LORD and to praise him for the splendour of his holiness as they went out at the head of the army, saying:
>
> 'Give thanks to the LORD,
>   for his love endures for ever.'

As they began to sing and praise, the LORD set ambushes against the men of Ammon and Moab and Mount Seir who were invading Judah, and they were defeated.

(2 Chron. 20:21–22)

Two important principles are illustrated by this account. First, God expects us to praise Him for the promises He gives us, without waiting to see them fulfilled. Second, praise offered in faith releases the supernatural intervention of God on our behalf. Briefly stated: faith begins to praise God before the promised victory, not merely after it.[2]

Similarly, it is as Paul and Silas, with backs lacerated from flogging, are praying and singing hymns to God, that an earthquake throws the prison doors open and their chains come loose (Acts 16:23–26).

I know of several situations where people have been praying for many years for members of their families to become believers. Often the breakthrough has come when they have stopped 'asking' and started 'praising' – praising God for their loved ones *just as they are*, and believing that God was working in spite of the outer circumstances. Let me encourage you to turn your prayers into praise – 'Sing, O barren woman'!

Forget not

When the psalmist says 'forget not all his benefits' (v.2) he is not referring to absent-mindedness, but to a deeper and subtler cause – pride.

- ■ When you have eaten and are satisfied, praise the LORD your God for the good land he has given you. Be careful that you do not forget the LORD your God, failing to observe his commands, his laws and his decrees that I am giving you this day. Otherwise, when you eat and are satisfied, when you build fine houses and settle down, and when your herds and flocks grow large and your silver and gold increase and all you have is multiplied, then your heart will become proud and you will forget the LORD your God, who brought you out of Egypt, out of the land of slavery ... You may say to yourself, 'My power and the strength of my hands have produced this wealth for me.' (Deut. 8:10–14, 17)

■ But Hezekiah's heart was proud and he did not respond to the kindness shown him; therefore the LORD's wrath was on him and on Judah and Jerusalem. (2 Chron. 32:25)

Our lack of thankfulness may signal either pride in our own achievements or a false view that we somehow deserved God's blessings. Alternatively, our lack of thankfulness may be due to some situation in our lives which we think God ought to change. The fact that He does not appear to have acted may block our thankfulness for other benefits we have received – we become full of self-pity, resentment, envy, anger or fear and these cloud our perspective. Ephesians 4:31 tells us to cleanse ourselves (through repentance) of all these things.

God's mercy

In verses 6 to 18 the psalmist changes from the singular to the plural – from God's blessings to the individual to His mercy for all His covenant people. He then uses the Exodus story as a case study to illustrate God's dealings with His people.

'No story surpasses the Exodus for a record of human

unworthiness: of grace abounding and "benefits forgot". Its mention in verse 7 reminds us of the sullen ingratitude God encounters in reply to the forgiving, healing and redeeming of which the opening verses sang.'[3]

The Exodus

'The LORD works righteousness and justice for all the oppressed' (Psa. 103:6) by providing a deliverer – Moses; by bringing them out of Egypt; by giving them the riches of the Egyptians and providing a safe route of travel (Exod. 13:17–18). 'He made known his ways to Moses, his deeds to the people of Israel …' (Psa. 103:7). How? Through His salvation, His protection, His guidance (the pillars of cloud and of fire), His provision (the manna and the quail), His destination (the promised land) and His Law (the Ten Commandments).

Given all these benefits you would think that thankfulness and praise would be the only possible response. Not so. The Israelites responded by complaining about the food (Num. 11:4–6); wishing they were back in Egypt (Num. 11:18); and making a golden calf to worship instead of God (Exod. 32:1–6). I find it all too easy to point out the speck in the eye of the Israelites and to fail to notice the plank in my own – only those of us who have never grumbled, never fantasised about how things might have been if we had taken a different path, and never looked to something or someone other than God to make our life work have any right to criticise them. Yet there is hope for us all, for God does not treat them or us as our sins deserve. As Exodus 34:4–8 and Psalm 103:8 put it: 'The LORD is compassionate and gracious, slow to anger, abounding in love.'

God's throne

'The Lord has established his throne in heaven, and his kingdom rules over all' (Psa. 103:19). Our God is not just our personal God, or Lord of His people, He is King of ALL! His dominion extends to every part of His creation. Although not all His creatures acknowledge His rule, He is still their King. David concludes this psalm by summoning the whole created order to praise their King. Firstly he addresses the angels (the mighty ones, God's hosts and servants) who do God's will, to join in this song of praise, then he calls on 'all his works everywhere' and finally, as at the beginning of this psalm, his own soul.

Our response

An appropriate response to this psalm is to remember and to praise. Remembrance is a choice and it is a discipline. One of my brothers has a poor memory for birthdays and some years mine would go by totally unacknowledged. It hurt. In the last few years he has always remembered my birthday. The change is not because his memory has suddenly improved but because he has taken the trouble to programme it into his computer diary. If we really want to remember God's benefits we will find ways of doing so. Remembering is easier when we have developed the habit of thankfulness. They say it takes 30 days to develop a habit, so if you were to spend the next month deliberately choosing to rehearse God's blessings to you every day, it would soon become natural.

Remembrance leads to praise! I became a Christian in my teens and in services at the local Methodist church sung some of the great hymns. One line in the hymn 'Come, thou fount of every blessing' mystified me: 'Here I raise my Ebenezer; Hither by thy help I'm come.'[4] What was my Ebenezer and how did I raise it? It wasn't until I read 1 Samuel 7:12 that I understood: 'Then Samuel took a stone and set it up between Mizpah and Shen. He named it Ebenezer, saying "Thus far has the LORD helped us."'

Samuel recognised that every victory over the enemy came from the Lord – every step forward we make in our spiritual life is a blessing from God. It is helpful to reflect back over our lives and think about all that the Lord has brought us through and raise our Ebenezer in thankfulness and praise. *'Praise the LORD, O my soul!'*

Questions for reflection

■ Note down all the things for which you want to thank God.

■ Why might you 'forget all His benefits'?

■ Write your own psalm of thanks to God and sing it to Him. (Note that God only requires a joyful noise – not a tuneful one!)

■ Praise God for one of your unsaved friends or relatives, just as he or she is, and thank God for being at work in his or her life.

■ Are there any areas of your life you need to bring before God in repentance, knowing that He is slow to anger and abounding in love?

■ What practical things can you do to help you to remember to be thankful?

■ Draw a picture that represents your spiritual or life journey and when you have finished it 'raise your Ebenezer'.

Notes
1. Adapted from an article in *Renewal*, October 1991.
2. Derek Prince, *Blessing or Curse – You can choose!* (Word Publishing, 1990), p.205.
3. Derek Kidner, *Psalms, Tyndale Old Testament Commentaries* (IVP, 1973), p.365.
4. Hymn by Robert Robinson, *Methodist Hymn Book* (1933, revised 1954).

National Distributors

UK: (and countries not listed below)
CWR, Waverley Abbey House, Waverley Lane, Farnham, Surrey GU9 8EP.
Tel: (01252) 784700 Outside UK +44 1252 784700

AUSTRALIA: CMC Australasia, PO Box 519, Belmont, Victoria 3216.
Tel: (03) 5241 3288

CANADA: Cook Communications Ministries, PO Box 98, 55 Woodslee Avenue, Paris, Ontario.
Tel: 1800 263 2664

GHANA: Challenge Enterprises of Ghana, PO Box 5723, Accra.
Tel: (021) 222437/223249 Fax: (021) 226227

HONG KONG: Cross Communications Ltd, 1/F, 562A Nathan Road, Kowloon.
Tel: 2780 1188 Fax: 2770 6229

INDIA: Crystal Communications, 10-3-18/4/1, East Marredpalli, Secunderabad – 500026,
Andhra Pradesh.
Tel/Fax: (040) 27737145

KENYA: Keswick Books and Gifts Ltd, PO Box 10242, Nairobi.
Tel: (02) 331692/226047 Fax: (02) 728557

MALAYSIA: Salvation Book Centre (M) Sdn Bhd, 23 Jalan SS 2/64, 47300 Petaling Jaya, Selangor.
Tel: (03) 78766411/78766797 Fax: (03) 78757066/78756360

NEW ZEALAND: CMC Australasia, PO Box 36015, Lower Hutt.
Tel: 0800 449 408 Fax: 0800 449 049

NIGERIA: FBFM, Helen Baugh House, 96 St Finbarr's College Road, Akoka, Lagos.
Tel: (01) 7747429/4700218/825775/827264

PHILIPPINES: OMF Literature Inc, 776 Boni Avenue, Mandaluyong City.
Tel: (02) 531 2183 Fax: (02) 531 1960

SINGAPORE: Armour Publishing Pte Ltd, Block 203A Henderson Road,
11–06 Henderson Industrial Park, Singapore 159546.
Tel: 6 276 9976 Fax: 6 276 7564

SOUTH AFRICA: Struik Christian Books, 80 MacKenzie Street, PO Box 1144, Cape Town 8000.
Tel: (021) 462 4360 Fax: (021) 461 3612

SRI LANKA: Christombu Books, 27 Hospital Street, Colombo 1.
Tel: (01) 433142/328909

TANZANIA: CLC Christian Book Centre, PO Box 1384, Mkwepu Street, Dar es Salaam.
Tel/Fax (022) 2119439

ZIMBABWE: Word of Life Books (Pvt) Ltd, Christian Media Centre, 8 Aberdeen Road, Avondale,
PO Box A480, Harare, Zimbabwe. Tel: (04) 333355 or 091301188

For email addresses, visit the CWR website: www.cwr.org.uk

CWR is a Registered charity – Number 294387

CWR is a limited company registered in England – Registration Number 1990308